M000203514

8-1-15

EARLY ADOPTER
RECOGNITION

In order to develop, write, and publish a book, an author needs the encouragement and enthusiasm that only a special group of people can provide. I call them Early Adopters—patrons who believe so much in an idea that they rally around it with early and significant support.

To my Early Adopters, thank you for helping me move Hyper from a vague concept to a physical (and digital) reality. I am forever grateful.

Toby George

Russ Karr

Matt McMahon

Chris Miladinovich

Navin Parmar

Donald Pavlinsky

Angel Smith

Craig Swen

Jim Torchia

Guy Vincent

PRAISE FOR **HYPER**

"Hyper leads you down an intelligent path to accelerated decision-making with simple, yet powerful methods that quickly align the business, establish priorities, gather requirements, and deliver results. It covers important concepts and strategies necessary for BI success and provides the kind of relevant and practical insight that only comes from years of experience."

Sri Hari Naidu Seepana
Analytics Manager
eBay Inc.

"A clear, insightful, and to-the-point strategy for making BI work. This is a must read for every BI professional."

Jeremy Jackson
Chief Executive Officer
simpleBI

"I finished a major BI requirements elicitation session just before reading Hyper. I thought that the process and rigor behind the book was compelling enough that I'm going to call key players back and redo it, this time using Greg's methodology. I realized that I made some serious misses without it. Really happy to get some clarity around this area of responsibility."

Roland Hess
Senior Technical Solutions Consultant
Google, Inc.

"We all know the principle, 'You can only manage what you can measure.' We also know that for speed and responsiveness, we need to push decision-making down in the organization. Somehow, though, we tend to overcomplicate the solution and waste a lot of time, energy, and opportunity in the process. Hyper brings us back to an important reality: to keep it simple, involve the whole team, and have the flexibility to iterate through a solution that delivers real value incrementally."

Kevin Deacon
Consultant, International Marketing and Business Strategy
Siemens Industry, Inc.

"Data fuels business, and only those firms able to quickly extract and utilize intelligence from their data assets will win in the 21st century. In Hyper, Steffine condenses decades of experience and lessons learned into a guide of tips and techniques business leaders can use to drive value from information."

Jay Zaidi
Managing Partner
AlyData

"While everyone talks about 'big data' and 'predictive analytics,' Hyper cuts through all of the unproductive 'hype' by providing a simple and effective framework to align, define, and deliver business intelligence in a quick and agile manner. Steffine's powerful set of guidelines on how to perform accelerated planning and execution are invaluable in helping any executive who needs actionable insight to support ongoing business transformation and change in today's global environment."

Tom De Winne
Vice President of Business Transformation
Pcubed

"When it comes to business intelligence, business and technical leaders often struggle to keep pace with and adapt to the ever-changing and complex business landscape in which they operate. Hyper helps by presenting a better approach to BI planning and execution—one that effectively addresses fundamental issues and yields impactful outcomes as a result. Well-written and well done."

Karan Talwar
Advisor, Pharmacy Analytics Center of Excellence
CVS Health

"I don't want 'data' at my fingertips. I want data that's transformed into relevant, timely, and easily accessible 'information' so I'm empowered to make faster and smarter business decisions. Hyper is a pragmatic guide that challenges business and IT to move beyond simply managing data to a place where they can quickly and routinely deliver actionable insight. This book is a must read for executives who want to use business intelligence as a competitive differentiator."

Gary Smelko
EVP Transportation and Terminals
Guttman Energy, Inc.

"For many people, business intelligence is all about technology. What I appreciate most about Hyper is its focus on business and the practical use of information for solving business problems. Steffine moves his readers methodically through a planning and execution process that ultimately delivers the capability an organization needs for quick, dynamic interpretation of information."

David Hanna
Senior Informatics Lead - Data Science Informatics
Aetna

"Hyper provides an insightful, thought-provoking look into the world of business intelligence, and it's sure to challenge many of the pre-conceived notions practitioners have about how to make BI work. In keeping with its name, Hyper is a fast-paced quick read that presents a cutting-edge BI planning and execution model."

Scott Cesare
BI Data Architect
Fortune 500 Regional Bank

"Now more than ever the C-Suite turns first to their BI experts to guide them through their most complex and important business decisions. Hyper is an exceptional, practical guide written for BI professionals who want to position themselves out in front of their organizations armed with real-time data, smart analytic processes, and ways to communicate complex information simply."

Blake R. Zenger
Chief Informatics Officer
Equity Healthcare (Blackstone)

"Hyper gets to the heart of BI success. The keys: stay close to the business and deliver value fast, even if you have to break some of the rules. This is a must-read guide for any self-respecting BI professional."

Wayne Eckerson
Founder and Principal Consultant
Eckerson Group

HYPER

Changing the way you think about, plan, and execute
Business Intelligence
for real results, real fast!

Gregory P. Steffine

Foreword by Boris Evelson

Sanderson™

Sanderson℠

Published by Sanderson Press, LLC
P.O. Box 1373, Aliquippa, Pennsylvania 15001-9998
United States

Hyper. Changing the way you think about, plan, and execute business intelligence for real results, real fast!

ISBN: 978-0-692-42308-0

Copyright ©2015 by Sanderson Press, LLC. All rights reserved. Printed in the United States of America. No part of this publication may be reproduced, stored in a retrieval system, or transmitted in any form or by any means, electronic, mechanical, photocopying, recording, scanning, or otherwise, except as permitted under Section 107 or 108 of the 1976 United States Copyright Act, without the prior written permission of the publisher. Submit written requests for permission to Permissions Department, Sanderson Press, LLC. P.O. Box 1373, Aliquippa, Pennsylvania 15001-9998.

Limit of Liability/Disclaimer of Warranty: While the publisher and author have used their best efforts in preparing this book, they make no representations or warranties with respect to the accuracy or completeness of the contents of this book and specifically disclaim any implied warranties of merchantability or fitness for a particular purpose.

The advice, strategies, and methods contained herein may not be suitable for your situation. You should consult with a professional where appropriate. Neither the publisher nor author shall be liable for any loss of profits or any other commercial damages, including but not limited to special, incidental, consequential, or other damages.

Neither the publisher nor the author has any material connection to the brands, products, or services mentioned in this book. The author only recommends products or services he has personally used or believes may add value to his readers. This disclosure is written is accordance with the Federal Trade Commission's 16 CFR, Part 255: "Guides Concerning the Use of Endorsements and Testimonials in Advertising."

The opinions expressed under *Praise for Hyper* do not represent an endorsement by the reviewers' respective employers. All referenced trademarks are the property of their respective owners.

Some content that appears in print may not be available in the electronic book. For simplicity, this book follows the tradition of using masculine pronouns to represent both male and female subjects.

DEDICATION

To Mary, my wife of 25 years. Without your encouragement and love, this book would not exist.

TABLE OF **CONTENTS**

FOREWORD

The Age Of The Customer Demands A New Approach To BI Planning and Execution

The power to define how business is won or lost has shifted into the hands of the digitally-empowered customer. We are living in what Forrester calls the Age of the Customer, and it has completely changed the BI equation.[1] Customers, armed with mobile phones and ubiquitous cloud-based access to nearly every vendor, product, service, and deal can now make instantaneous buying decisions and wield incredible influence—all at the click of a button on their mobile device. This makes winning and retaining customers the number one business priority, and the ability to almost instantaneously react to ever-changing customer demands a new competitive differentiator. Supporting our long held belief, Forrester Research now has quantitative proof that business can only thrive amid ever-accelerating market changes and dynamics when it's supported by information and process agility.[2] But what does that mean in pragmatic and actionable terms for business and IT professionals working on BI initiatives?

First, Forrester believes that, in the Age of the Customer, business and IT professionals must focus on supporting business agility in order to make BI work.[3]

They should:

- **Treat their business users just like customers—even when they are wrong, they are right.** Forrester finds that agile organizations make decisions differently by embracing a new, more grass-roots-based management approach.[4] In addition to top-down BI requirements mandated by management, employees in the trenches are the ones who are in close touch with customer problems, market shifts, and process inefficiencies. These workers are often in the best position to understand challenges and opportunities and to make decisions that improve the business. It is only when responses to change come from within—from these highly-aware and empowered employees—do enterprises become agile, competitive, and successful. And it is only when technology professionals start listening to all business stakeholders, not just senior managers, that a more realistic picture of an effective and efficient BI environment becomes clear and actionable.

- **Embrace business agility, which sometimes trumps a single version of the truth.** A modern, agile world is not binary. A single version of the truth is relative to who's asking the question, and other contexts. If it's good and timely and addresses relevant customer data needs, then that version of the truth takes higher priority in the Age of the Customer.

Enable business agility with agile BI best practices and platforms. Agile enterprises must gather customer and market knowledge and rapidly incorporate it into decisions. In order to support and promote business agility, enterprise knowledge workers must be empowered with easy access to agile, flexible, and responsive enterprise business intelligence tools and applications.[5]

Second, Forrester recommends that business learns from the mistakes many have already made in their long and perilous BI journeys and, instead, focus on jump-starting BI development cycles with:

- **Rapid prototypes.** Most modern BI platforms have desktop or cloud-based sandbox capabilities, where business users together with their technology professional counterparts can often build rapid prototypes faster than it takes to collect and document requirements on paper. In-memory based platforms that do not require long cycles and database administrators (DBAs) to build data models are especially handy.

- **Rapidly deploying and learning from proofs of concepts (POCs).** Even the top BI experts can seldom be successful without some trial and error. In order to succeed quickly, Forrester recommends first learning how to fail quickly. Rapid prototypes achieve just that purpose—they allow one to fail quickly, learn from the mistakes (before they get noticed or too many resources get wasted), get progressively closer to the ultimate objective, and then demonstrate value with a stable POC which indeed delivers on the original promise.

- **No more than two weeks apart from tangible, usable deliverables.** Just like in the story of Goldilocks and the Three Bears, Forrester often finds that a few days may be too soon and a few months may be too long between tangible BI deliverables. Two weeks seems to be just right. Indeed, a few leading management consulting firms are now building such a two-week cycle into their standard BI project plan templates.

Forrester recommends our BI Playbook and other relevant Forrester BI research documents to help your organization with strategic planning, establishing your vision, and high-level roadmaps; then look to Hyper for the next level of tactical and operational detail necessary to kick-start and reenergize your effort at building a responsive, agile, and flexible BI capability.[6]

Boris Evelson
Vice President and Principal Analyst
Forrester Research, Inc.

PREFACE

For far too many organizations, information remains an untapped resource. It was that way when I began my career in 1986, and it's still that way today—despite our desire to be "smarter" about how we conduct business, despite massive investments we've made over the years in technological advancements around data, and despite the knowledge that "business analytics is the critical competency of the new age."[1]

As a long-time consultant, I've had the privilege of working with companies both big and small—from the Fortune 500 to mid-market growth organizations. One thing I've consistently noticed is that, regardless of company size or industry, organizations struggle to leverage information for competitive advantage because of the way they think about, plan, and execute their BI initiatives. My former colleagues at Deloitte call it the "inertia of good intentions"—personal behavior created by "institutional routines, obligations, and pressures"[2] that actually hold many back (unsuspectingly) from delivering the kind of value their organizations need when they need it.

The vision of every organization is to create value. Hyper is intended to help you think about, plan, and execute BI differently so you can close the gap between that vision and the unfortunate reality that most companies face.

Hyper is all about "speed-to-information"—providing business leaders with the insight they need to take action before their decision windows close.

This book is an extension of my work, so in it you'll find the same ideas, methods, and tools I've developed and effectively used over the course of my career to help build smarter organizations. Hyper is not a technical resource on how to architect, deploy, or govern a BI solution. It assumes you already know how to do that. Rather, it shows you how you can accelerate the value of business intelligence through organizational alignment, right requirements, and the exploitation of quick wins.

Hyper is organized into five content-rich sections along with an appendix of valuable resources I reference on a routine basis.

Section 1 – Understanding BI

Section 2 – The Imperatives for Success

Section 3 – Methods to Accelerate Planning

Section 4 – Ways to Accelerate Execution

Section 5 – Beyond Planning and Execution

Appendix – Recommended Resources

You'll also find throughout this book a liberal use of graphics to help highlight key concepts and deepen your understanding of them. Some of the concepts will be new to you. Others will be familiar.

Build on the ideas presented in this book and make them your own. Customize them to suit your needs and the needs of your organization in order to deliver BI in a Hyper way.

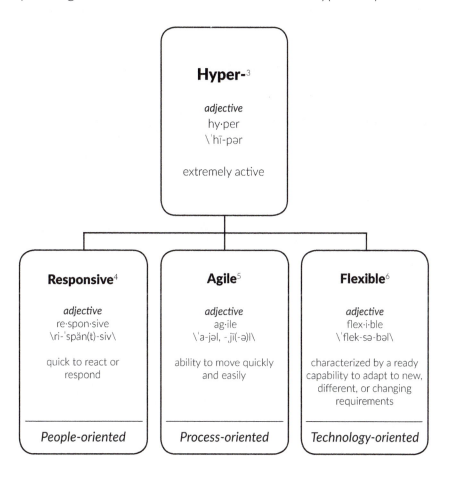

Lastly, it's always tough naming a book. I picked the prefix "Hyper" because it most accurately denotes the energy and action every business requires from the people, processes, and technology that underpin an effective BI competency. In my experience, BI works best when people are Hyper-responsive, processes are Hyper-agile, and technology is Hyper-flexible.

Gregory P. Steffine
Business Intelligence Strategist and Solution Delivery Leader

ACKNOWLEDGEMENTS

To my clients, colleagues, and friends

Thank you for enabling me to do what I love.

To my family

Alongside a busy career, this book consumed nearly every other moment of my waking (and sleeping) time; thank you for your patience and unconditional support.

To Sandy

Thank you for being such a loyal friend.

To Bob, Bruce, Ida, and my entire publishing team

Thank you for your interest in my work and your careful attention to detail.

To Rock, Ryan, and the team at UPMC

Thank you for looking after my health.

To Joseph

Thank you for keeping me grounded, focused, and sane.

To my Lord and Savior, Jesus Christ

Thank you for the promise of John 3:16 and the assurance of Jeremiah 29:11; I pray that my work is honoring to you.

SECTION 1
UNDERSTANDING BI

Information is the one thing an organization creates that its competitors can't replicate. So write Mark Hurd and Lars Nyberg in their book, *The Value Factor: How Global Leaders Use Information for Growth and Competitive Advantage.*[1] Business intelligence—often referred to simply as "BI"—is the use of information to create and maximize value.

In this section, you'll learn that value creation is the primary role of every organization. I introduce you to the BI Value Chain and the Value Enablers that support the creation of value. And I describe the very problem most organizations encounter when they try to make BI work.

CHAPTER 1
VALUE CREATION

“ Value creation is a corporation's *raison d'être*, the ultimate measure by which it is judged.[1] ”

- The Economist

VALUE CREATION

The vision of every organization is to create value. In fact, value creation is the primary focus of managerial activity.[2] That's what business professors Prahalad and Ramaswamy write in their book, *The Future of Competition*. And who doesn't know a manager, regardless of industry or company size, who isn't under intense pressure to do just that?

This mandate to create value is the primary reason corporate leaders consistently rate business intelligence (BI) as one of their top investment priorities.[3] They recognize the instrumental role information plays in driving innovation. They understand the significance of information in creating differentiation. And they know the importance of information in monitoring and managing performance. In short, they rely on information to drive more effective decision-making. For these business leaders, business intelligence enables value creation.

Organizations create value by effectively meeting the unique and diverse interests of their stakeholders. "Every business has stakeholders," writes University of Virginia professor Ed Freeman. In his book, *Stakeholder Theory: State of the Art*, he defines them as "groups and individuals who can affect or are affected by business."[4] In Figure 1, I present a simplistic view of three stakeholder groups along with some common expectations of value.

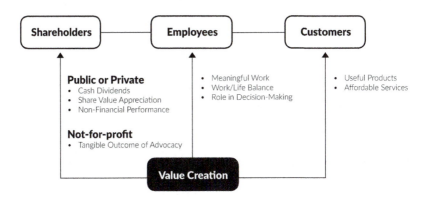

Figure 1 - Value Expectations of Stakeholder Groups

- Shareholders are investors—of time, money, or both. They expect value through cash dividends, share value appreciation, and improvement in non-financial performance measures. In the case of not-for-profit organizations, stakeholders are called members, donors, clients, and partners. To them, value takes the form of some tangible outcome associated with the entity's advocacy effort—something Harvard professor Michael Porter calls "social value."[5]

- To employees—those who represent the organization and conduct its operation—value consists of meaningful work and associated opportunities for professional growth, a role in the decision-making process, and the ability to effectively monitor and manage personal performance.

- As for customers, they expect value in the form of quality products or services the market finds both useful and affordable.

An organization's survival ultimately rests on how well it creates and maximizes value for its stakeholder groups, and business intelligence plays an instrumental role. But value creation doesn't happen by chance. It's the result of smart, fact-based decisions made possible by a decision support hierarchy I call the BI Value Chain.

CHAPTER 2
THE BI VALUE CHAIN

" Creating value is taking what you know and turning it into action in order to achieve a desired business outcome. "

THE BI VALUE CHAIN

The BI Value Chain (Figure 2) is a series of business principles that, when properly linked, enables business leaders (and all knowledge workers for that matter) to harness the power of information in order to create and maximize value.

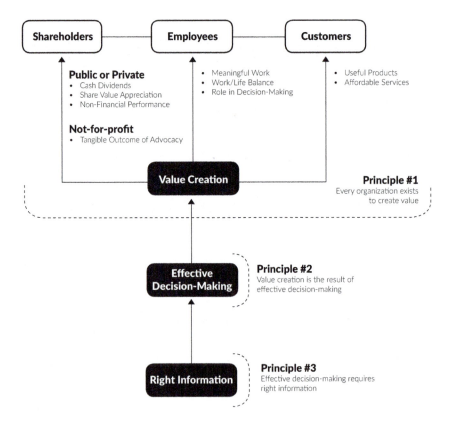

Figure 2 - BI Value Chain

Principle #1 - Every organization exists to create value.

Now more than ever, business leaders face increasing pressure to drive innovation, differentiation, and performance. It's the result of growing complexity, mounting risk, and rising uncertainty around doing business in a demanding, oversupplied, and increasingly price-sensitive place called the new economy. When business leaders talk value, they use action words like increase, reduce, and strengthen; grow, shrink, and improve; maximize, minimize, and revitalize. Creating value, writes author and business advisor Jill Konrath, is all about movement.[1] In "Lessons from change: Findings from the market," EY says that high-performance organizations share a common agenda when it comes to creating movement, and that includes "accelerating decision-making and execution."[2]

Principle #2 - Value creation is the result of effective decision-making.

It was 1999 when Klaus Schwab, best known as the founder and executive chairman of the World Economic Forum, said "We've moved from a world where the big eat the small to a world where the fast eat the slow."[3] Our world is obsessed with speed, and every business needs to think and move faster than its competition if it's going to survive. But "Being faster doesn't mean being out of breath," write Jason Jennings and Laurence Haughton in their book, *It's Not the Big That Eat the Small...It's the Fast that Eat the Slow: How to Use Speed As a Competitive Tool in Business.*

"It means being smarter."[4] And it's one of the reasons business leaders recognize that value creation ultimately depends on effective decision-making. For high-performance companies, it's both fast and focused. And its level of effectiveness is what ultimately separates the best from the rest. As EY points out, using data insight and analysis for faster and smarter decision-making is one of the most significant differences between top performers and those who want to be top performers.

These are the organizations which gain benefit from what marketing and strategic management professionals call the "first-mover advantage." It's the notion that speed-to-market provides a business with a competitive advantage over its rivals. It's the business world's equivalent to "the early bird gets the worm." First-mover types make fast, focused decisions that create value because they are empowered with speedy access to information. But not just any information.

Principle #3 - Effective decision-making requires the right information.

Just as high-performance automobiles require the right fuels to power their engines, business leaders require the right information to power the right decisions. I like the analogy because it conveys an important truth to our "keep everything" business culture: not all data matters.

Only leaders informed with the right information (not those drowning in data) have the ability to take their organizations beyond the simple capacity to survive to a place where they can thrive. Right information provides the kind of insight or "informed intelligence" decision-makers need to confidently and consistently create business impact.

Experience and observation indicate that organizations with the ability to quickly convert data to information to business value enjoy a significant competitive advantage over those who can't. It's a result of the BI Value Chain at work.

CHAPTER 3
VALUE ENABLERS

" At a time when firms in many industries offer similar products and use comparable technologies, business processes are among the last remaining points of differentiation.[1] "

- Thomas H. Davenport

VALUE ENABLERS

The idea of the value chain is based on the process view of organisations."[2] This concept was first popularized by Harvard Business School professor Michael Porter in his best-selling book, *Competitive Advantage: Creating and Sustaining Superior Performance.* Porter identified a series of generic, interrelated activities common to most organizations—all of which are important to creating sustainable competitive advantage.[3]

VALUE ENABLER	FOCUS
• Processes to Plan and Execute	• The organization's mission, strategies, objectives, and plans that drive business execution in order to compete and make money
• Processes to Monitor and Refine	• The use of and reporting and analytics to evaluate the past, monitor the present, and predict the future
• Information Assets to Enable and Empower	• The organization's information model, physical reporting structures, and source systems; and the underlying architecture and information management practices that support them

An expanded view of the BI Value Chain (Figure 3) depicts a series of generic business processes—what I call Value Enablers—that underpin an organization's decision support system. The extent to which these enablers interrelate ultimately determines how well an organization uses information to manage, optimize, and innovate.

Smart organizations achieve closed-loop interaction between value enablers, and they do so by adhering to three specific Value-Enabling Rules:

Value-Enabling Rule #1 - Data must be relevant

"Nobody needs to be flooded with useless data," says Jeff Chasney, Senior Vice President of Strategic Planning and Chief Information Officer for CKE Restaurants.[4] Effective decision support begins with the identification of data that helps strengthen the decision-making process so that business leaders can make a real difference.

Value-Enabling Rule #2 - Information must be meaningful

Meaningful information is useful information. It's accurate, consistently defined, and relevant to daily behavior. Information is useful when it helps you run your business effectively, says Jane Griffin, Managing Director of Deloitte Analytics Canada.[5] But, as Chasney notes, "If you're just presenting information that's neat and nice but doesn't evoke a decision or impart important knowledge, then it's [just] noise."[6]

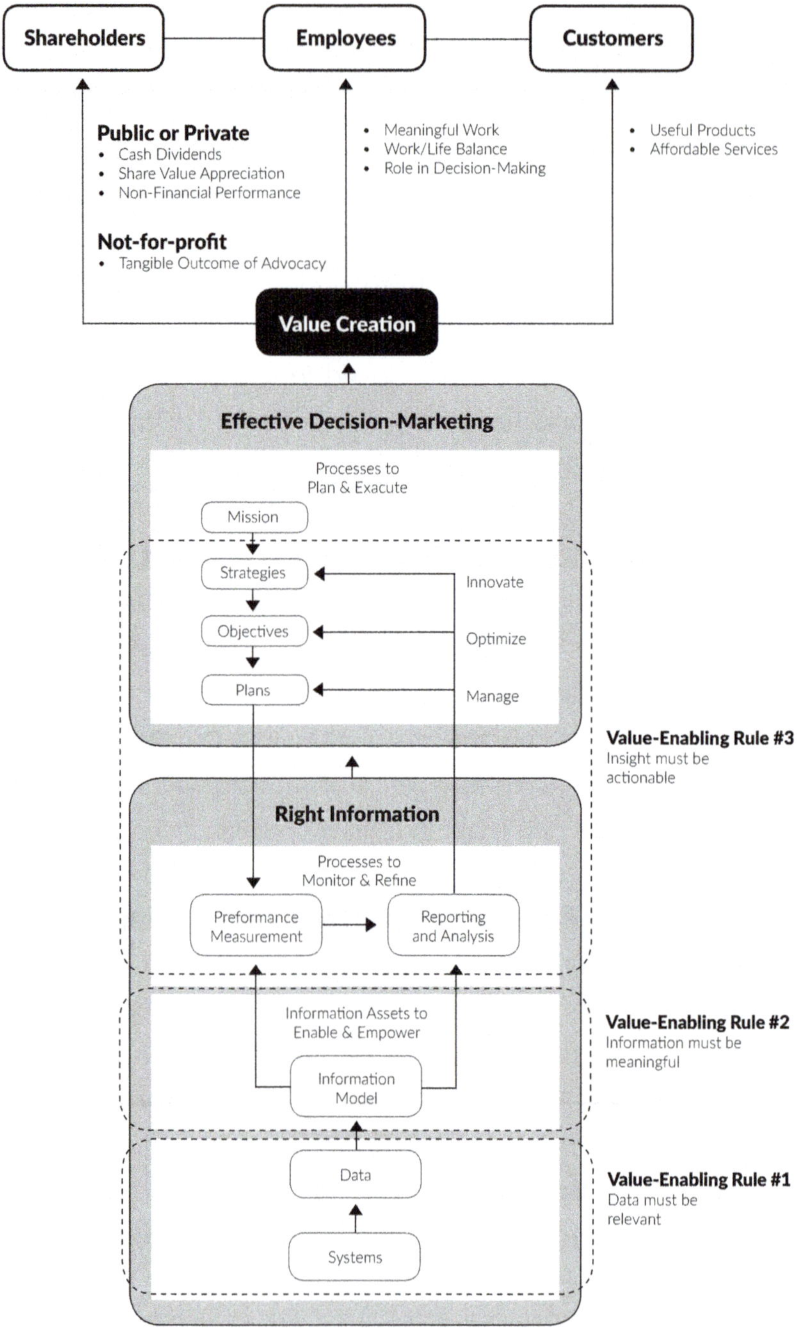

Shareholders — **Employees** — **Customers**

Public or Private
- Cash Dividends
- Share Value Appreciation
- Non-Financial Performance

Not-for-profit
- Tangible Outcome of Advocacy

- Meaningful Work
- Work/Life Balance
- Role in Decision-Making

- Useful Products
- Affordable Services

Value Creation

Effective Decision-Marketing

Processes to
Plan & Exacute

Mission

Strategies ← Innovate

Objectives ← Optimize

Plans ← Manage

Right Information

Processes to
Monitor & Refine

Preformance Measurement → Reporting and Analysis

Information Assets to
Enable & Empower

Information Model

Data

Systems

Value-Enabling Rule #3
Insight must be actionable

Value-Enabling Rule #2
Information must be meaningful

Value-Enabling Rule #1
Data must be relevant

Figure 3 - Expanded View of BI Value Chain

Value-Enabling Rule #3 - Insight must be actionable

Information becomes insightful when it imparts important knowledge relevant to the organization's strategies, objectives, or plans. Actionable means the insight is easily understood and delivered in a method and timeframe that provides an opportunity for the decision-maker to act.

Problem is, for every organization that empowers decision-makers with relevant data, meaningful information, and actionable insight, many more fail to fully capitalize on BI's promise of enabling real and meaningful business impact. It's a pervasive problem, and one that touches companies of every shape, size, and industry.

CHAPTER 4
THE PROBLEM WITH BI

" Many companies struggle to transform information into usable insights, actions, and results.[1] "

- Jeanne Harris

THE PROBLEM WITH BI

In *Results-Based Leadership,* authors Ulrich, Zenger, and Smallwood write that "Leaders who aren't getting results aren't truly leading."[2] Most managers instinctively know this. Successful ones understand the BI Value Chain, and they rely on having the right information at the right time in order to support strategic, tactical, and operational decision-making. They are results-based leaders: managers driven by the "need to know." They recognize the instrumental role information plays in creating value. They see information as the lifeblood of the organization, and they use it to confidently and consistently lead by delivering results that count. Unfortunately, the results-based leader isn't a common leader. More than two decades after Gartner Research Fellow Howard Dresner coined the term "business intelligence,"[3] too many organizations and the decision-makers who run them still struggle to get BI right.

In an effort to help executives lead, the BI industry has spent the last couple of decades making data access easier, analytic capability more comprehensive, and platforms more scalable. Yet, despite pouring billions of dollars into BI initiatives, executives still come-up empty-handed when they reach for the information they need to make well-informed decisions. They live in what futurist and author Thornton May calls the "analytical dark ages."[4] Executives are simply unable to fully capitalize on BI's promise of turning actionable insight into real business value because information they need is either limited or missing entirely from the decision-making process. Their BI Value Chains are broken—the kind of result you can expect when business and IT fail to adequately address four primary challenges associated with BI planning and execution:

Challenge #1
Organizations gets enamored with technology and lose business perspective

Challenge #2
Organizations overcomplicate the BI effort

Challenge #3
Organizations fail to evangelize

Challenge #4
Organizations don't manage their BI initiatives to expected business outcomes

The good news is that there are practical steps you can take and techniques you can use to effectively address these challenges in order to build a BI competency that really works.

SECTION 2
THE IMPERATIVES FOR SUCCESS

The challenges organizations face when they attempt to build an effective BI competency must be addressed because they battle against the organizational alignment, collaboration, and trust that's ultimately required for success.

In this section, I introduce you to the actionable steps you can take to overcome the challenges with BI in order to reconnect and strengthen the links of a broken BI Value Chain.

CHAPTER 5
ADDRESSING THE PROBLEM WITH BI

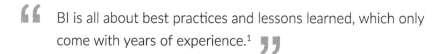 BI is all about best practices and lessons learned, which only come with years of experience.[1]

- Boris Evelson

ADDRESSING THE PROBLEM WITH BI

The Imperatives for Success represent four actionable steps you can take to effectively address the challenges associated with BI planning and execution. I call them "imperatives" because they are "must-haves" for BI success. In the table that follows, I present each imperative under the primary challenge it addresses, along with its purpose and expected outcome.

The Problem with BI	Challenge #1 Organizations get enamored with technology and lose business perspective	Challenge #2 Organizations overcomplicate the BI effort
The Imperative for Success	Actionable Step #1 UNIFY	Actionable Step #2 SIMPLIFY
Purpose	In order to make BI work, business and IT must be unified around a series of fundamental BI principles, including how decision-makers intend to use information to create and maximize value.	BI works when the process to move from great idea to actionable insight is fast and focused. This step educates business and IT stakeholders on how to "keep things simple" when it comes to development and execution.
Business Outcome	Organizational alignment	Rapid time-to-value
Covered In	Chapter 6	Chapter 7

Challenge #3	**Challenge #4**
Organizations fail to evangelize	Organizations don't proactively manage their BI initiatives to expected business outcomes

Actionable Step #3	**Actionable Step #4**
AMPLIFY	QUALIFY

It's the alignment of an aware, knowledgeable, and engaged business community that ultimately helps to transform business through more effective decision-making.	BI works when it helps deliver the insight leaders expect when they expect it. Smart organizations commit themselves to proactively monitoring and evaluating BI performance and then adjusting accordingly.

BI adoption and momentum	Evolving BI maturity and decision-making effectiveness

Chapter 8	Chapter 9

CHAPTER 6
UNIFY

" In the province of the mind, what one believes to be true either is true or becomes true.[1] "

- Dr. John C. Lilly

UNIFY

What we believe influences how we behave, so unifying your organization begins with aligning many unique and often divergent perspectives on business intelligence. It's important that all stakeholders have a correct understanding of BI fundamentals—what I call Unifying Principles—before the organization embarks on any business intelligence initiative. That's because organizational alignment has a direct impact on BI adoption, and erroneous perceptions can lead your efforts astray by diverting your attention, frustrating stakeholders, and sapping your budget.

Unifying Principle #1 - BI has nothing to do with technology
Business intelligence is about business, not technology. Sure, technology helps make it work, but the value of any BI initiative is ultimately driven—not by the sophistication of your reporting tools, the number of dashboards you've deployed, or the power of your servers—but by the insight it provides and the impact it helps create. After all, BI has been technology- and infrastructure-driven almost from inception; yet, in far too many cases, it still doesn't meet the information needs of senior management.[2] That's not to say technology isn't important. "You need to establish your vision for your business intelligence strategy before you bring technology into the conversation," says Boris Evelson, principal analyst with Forrester Research and lead author of the study, "It's Time to Reinvent Your BI Strategy."[3]

A capable hardware and software environment is necessary if an organization wants to compete on analytics.[4] Just don't get enamored with technology; instead, focus your attention on getting the information right. Let business pain determine technology need. And ignore vendors who try to convince you that the BI "promised land" is simply one more purchase away. The reality is, when it comes to making BI successful, technology is low on the "gotta have it" list.[5]

Unifying Principle #2 - Not all data matters

Albert Einstein once said, "Not everything that counts can be counted and not everything that can be counted counts."[6] It's a truism our "keep everything" business culture has a tough time embracing. Today, our ability to store data has outstripped our ability to use it[7]—evidence that more data doesn't necessarily mean more informed decisions. We live in an era of information overload. So now, more than ever, it's important to focus. But it's important to focus on things that make a difference, say authors Newt Gingrich and Nancy Desmond. "Lions have to distinguish between antelopes and chipmunks," they write. "If [the lions] spend their time on the wrong thing, they will starve to death."[8] Decision-makers face the same harsh reality in business. Fact is, the only data that matters is the data that feeds the organization's appetite for the right information. Forget about everything else.

Unifying Principle #3 – BI is not a project

Business intelligence is a "business initiative," not a "technology project." That is, it is an ongoing effort to improve the organization's decision-making capability in order to create and maximize value. It has no finish line. That's because the definition of "the right information" changes as the organization evolves. The only way you can continue to effectively plan, execute, monitor, and refine your business operation is to ensure your BI capability keeps pace.

Unifying Principle #4 – Attitude is everything

Our attitude influences our actions and shapes how others see us. Zig Ziglar once said that "Your attitude, not your aptitude, will determine your altitude."[9] The right attitude is a prerequisite for effective collaboration and a must-have for creating the kind of cross-functional alignment you need for BI success. Make success your passion. Dedicate yourself to exceeding your customers' expectations. Pride yourself on making your colleagues some of the best decision-makers in the world. Treat your company's bottom line like it's your bottom line. Say what you mean and mean what you say. Do whatever it takes to get the job done on-budget, on-time, every time. And always strive to do it once, do it right, and make it last. Remember what successful businessman and philanthropist W. Clement Stone wrote about people. "There is little difference in people, but the little difference makes a big difference. The little difference is attitude."[10] Nothing spurs innovative thinking like BI. Done well, it can move business leaders to action: the kind of action that literally transforms the way an organization delivers value.

But creating and sustaining a BI-enabled environment of fact-based decision-making requires transformational thinking—a willingness to think outside-the-box that is driven by a "can do" attitude. Authors of *The Art of Transformation* suggest we "Approach new ideas by saying, 'yes, if' rather than 'no, because.'"[11] It's this kind of thinking that leads to actionable intelligence.

In Section 3, I describe a series of techniques I use to effectively align business and IT stakeholders around the vision for and practical implementation of business intelligence.

CHAPTER 7
SIMPLIFY

" Any intelligent fool can make things bigger, more complex....
It takes a touch of genius—and a lot of courage—to move in
the opposite direction.[1] "

- E.F. Schumacher

SIMPLIFY

Complexity is wreaking havoc on business. One study conducted by the Warwick Business School looked at the world's two hundred largest companies and found they were wasting over a billion dollars a year resulting from, among other things, overly complex business processes.[2]

Organizations unwittingly overcomplicate BI, too. Avoidable complexity often arises from poor communication between business and IT, from practitioners trying to do too much (and taking way too long in the process), from project teams over-architecting solutions, and from project leaders micromanaging the effort.

"Simple is smart," writes Alan Siegel and Irene Etzkorn, authors of *Simple: Conquering the Crisis of Complexity.*[3] BI works when the process of moving from great idea to actionable insight is fast and focused. Here are the top priorities for keeping things simple.

Keep It Simple Priority #1 - Create alliances

Now more than ever, CEOs rely on CIOs to drive an organization's "value-creation" agenda, and that makes effective collaboration between business and IT absolutely critical to BI success.[4] It is vital that stakeholders work overtime to bridge the communication, trust, and understanding gap that represents today's business-IT relationship.

Once seen as a strategic enabler, many business leaders view IT as nothing more than a roadblock to the kind of speed and responsiveness they need to compete. On the other hand, IT leaders often see business as unreasonable and unwilling to accept the kind of thoughtful rigor required to make systems perform and last. The objective is to get business and IT to see eye-to-eye. BI works when business and IT work together.

Keep It Simple Priority #2 - Crawl, walk, run

While executives want better information for management decision-making, many find themselves constrained by practical budget and priority limitations. After all, business intelligence solutions aren't cheap. And while those of us who design, build, and deploy them like to believe there's no greater investment priority for the business, this isn't always the case. In fact, there is always competition for an organization's financial resources. One of the best approaches for securing executive buy-in to BI is "incremental development"; that is, building or expanding your reporting and analytics capability over time, one step at a time. Executives embrace this approach for a couple of good reasons: 1) it helps minimize exposure and risk; and 2) it enables them to use demonstrated value as justification for continued investment. You can't boil the ocean, so don't overcomplicate your BI effort by taking on so much that you fail to deliver quickly. The crawl-walk-run approach is about dividing and conquering—simplifying an otherwise complex process in order to achieve incremental progress that demonstrates real value.

Keep It Simple Priority #3 - Start with existing technology

Most organizations have already made significant investments in business intelligence tools and related infrastructure including the development of intellectual capital that only comes with experience and time. When building your BI capability, always start with existing technology. Prove that it can't or won't work before requesting additional funds for new tools or infrastructure. And remember: technology is rarely the reason for a broken BI Value Chain.

Keep It Simple Priority #4 - Focus on business enablement

The speed of business is only increasing. So, when it comes to providing decision-makers with the information they need to do their jobs, rapid time-to-results is absolutely critical. Firms need to adapt their governance frameworks, technology infrastructures, and tools so they can strike the right balance between maintaining control and enabling the business to get on with its job.[5] Create an environment that enables you to respond quickly to business needs. Build and deliver according to lightweight standards established by IT, then integrate the new capability into your enterprise environment following a pre-determined, agreed-upon process.

Keep It Simple Priority #5 - Don't forget governance

Governance aligns the right people, processes, and technology required to integrate, secure, optimize, and utilize an organization's information assets. Rather than trying to make governance a standalone initiative, incorporate it as an essential part of every business intelligence engagement.

The key is to implement just the right amount of governance needed to support the incremental development and utilization of your BI capability.

In Chapter 20, I discuss specific ways you can execute in a quick and nimble fashion.

CHAPTER 8
AMPLIFY

" Left unattended, the culture of most organizations will marginalize a BI initiative to the point of limited (and unacceptable) return. "

AMPLIFY

It's been my experience that skeptics and naysayers fill the ranks of most organizations. You know them. They like the status quo. They resist change. They make comments like "We've been down this road before" and "I'll believe it when I see it." At best, they're tough-minded "demanders of proof" willing to believe if you only show them the way. At worst, they're obstructionists who can unwittingly prevent your business intelligence initiative from yielding expected returns.

Dr. Mary Lippitt, an internationally-recognized authority on leading for results and author of the book, *The Leadership Spectrum: Six Business Priorities That Get Results*, calls them "members of the 'B' team: 'I'll be here when [the initiative] starts and I'll be here when it ends. I will just wait it out until it passes. No reason to really get on board.'"[1] Dr. Lippitt recognizes the critical role culture plays in determining the success or failure of any initiative. And rightfully so. "[Peter] Drucker knew the power of culture," she says, "and [he] captured it with his statement that 'culture eats strategy for breakfast.'"[2]

You can avoid the negative impact of skeptics and naysayers as well as a culture of mistrust by establishing organizational awareness and building excitement around your BI initiative.

To amplify means to evangelize. In his book, *Selling the Dream,* Guy Kawasaki describes evangelism as "the process of convincing people to believe in your idea as much as you do."[3] When it comes to BI, sell the dream! Al Parisian, CIO of the Montana State Fund and member of the Millbrook Executive Council, says to publicize, applaud, and celebrate your success. "When an executive uses BI to make a successful tactical move or scores a marketing win," he writes, "the whole company should hear about it."[4] Publicize and celebrate success. It helps to build the momentum and buy-in you need to drive BI adoption.

Kim Gordon, one of the country's leading marketing experts, says "Everyone in your company has the power to spread the good word about your business. The key is to have them all focus on a unified, motivational message."[5] The same holds true for internal, mission-critical initiatives like business intelligence. Passion is contagious. BI evangelists have the power to educate, inform, and motivate in ways that can yield long-lasting and dramatic change.

I discuss ways to socialize, market, and sell your initiative in Chapter 21.

CHAPTER 9
QUALIFY

  " If a business intelligence solution can't help you make sounds decisions about your company's future—easily, reliably, and at every level of the organization—it's neither good business nor intelligent.[1] **"**

- James Goodnight, Ph.D.

QUALIFY

Studies continue to illustrate broad dissatisfaction with business intelligence, with almost a third of BI projects failing to deliver on business objectives.[2] Why is that? Gartner's "Predicts 2012: business intelligence still subject to non-technical challenges" report points to a lack of business alignment, skills deficit, and reliance on vendor hype as some of the culprits.[3] Other reports, like the Ness Technologies Market Pulse Study, attribute underperformance to data-centric pain points like quality, integration, and access.[4] Do a simple search of the Internet and you'll find a host of sites providing a myriad of reasons why BI projects fail. It's no wonder the overall BI adoption rate today remains virtually unchanged from 2005.[5]

The real problem with BI adoption is that few organizations qualify success, and fewer still proactively monitor and measure BI performance against evolving end-user expectations. Too often practitioners build and deliver a reporting and analytics capability and then think the work is done.

Understand that business intelligence is a journey—a process of continuous improvement meant to adapt and evolve so that it can ultimately support an intelligent response to an ever-changing and dynamic business environment. Fact is, what decision-makers need to monitor and evaluate the business today won't be the same tomorrow.

Did you know that 80% of NASA's rockets require multiple mid-course corrections to arrive at their intended target?[6] "The same [holds] true with organizations," says Dr. Mary Lippitt, award-winning author and change management expert. "Only with active monitoring and adjustment will any plan succeed."[7]

The purpose of the Qualify Imperative is to ensure you focus adequate attention on active monitoring, evaluation, and adjustment of your organization's business intelligence capability so that it is always aligned with business need and always responsive to stakeholder expectations.

CHAPTER 10
THE IMPORTANCE OF COLLABORATION

" Despite the evidence to the contrary, we still tend to think of achievement in terms of the Great Man or Great Woman, instead of the Great Group.[1] "

- Warren Bennis

THE IMPORTANCE OF COLLABORATION

Ken Blanchard, management expert and co-author of *The One Minute Manager®*, once said, "None of us is as smart as all of us."[2] He speaks to the incredible value of collaboration—the synergy that results when we move beyond the ego-centric individual to what Warren Bennis calls "the Great Group." To borrow a phrase from Adam Richardson, Assistant VP of Strategy and Marketing at global innovation firm Frog Design, "Collaboration is a team sport."[3]

Organizations rely on collaboration to increase business value. Studies indicate that effective collaboration impacts productivity, quality, innovation, customer service, and financial performance. "As a general rule, global companies that collaborate better, perform better," says Dr. Jaclyn Kostner, best-selling author of the book, *Virtual Leadership*. "Those that collaborate less, do not perform as well. It's just that simple."[4] A 2006 McKinsey Quarterly report confirms Dr. Kostner's assertion. It concludes that an industry's top performers excel because they collaborate better than their peers. In short, better collaboration leads to better performance.[5]

That certainly reflects my experience with business intelligence. Regardless of organization size, BI only works when business and IT work together. Both have important roles to play. "In order for a firm to become an analytical competitor," writes Thomas H. Davenport and Jeanne G. Harris, authors of *Competing on Analytics: The New Science of Winning,* "the demand for and supply of data and analysis must be in alignment."[6] Business stakeholders drive demand. They require relevant data, meaningful information, and actionable insight that enable more effective operational, tactical, and strategic decision-making. It's the job of IT to supply it—to find it, understand it, transform it, and stage it for fast, easy consumption. Effective collaboration ensures the delivery of a business intelligence capability is always aligned with business requirements and always responsive to stakeholder expectations.

"Supply and demand" is the place where business and IT meet. Problem is, it's also the place where you need to overcome language barriers, politics, and personal agendas that often fight against collaboration and result in something I call The Understanding Gap (Figure 4).[7]

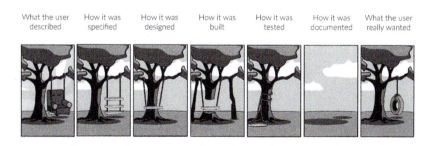

| What the user described | How it was specified | How it was designed | How it was built | How it was tested | How it was documented | What the user really wanted |

Figure 4 - The Understanding Gap

The purpose of collaboration is to get business and IT aligned around BI requirements so you can avoid rogue business units acting as IT shops in order to get their jobs done and IT shops attempting to support the business by building "enterprise data landfills."[8] Neither situation is good for a company, but it's what happens when BI professionals fail to bridge-the-gap between "what the user describes" and "what the user really wants."

In Chapter 11, I introduce a proven framework you can use to (finally) unify business and IT around a shared understanding of business intelligence requirements that support value creation.

SECTION 3
METHODS TO ACCELERATE PLANNING

Planning is preparation for action. Delivering data that is relevant, information that is meaningful, and insight that is actionable requires planning that's both fast and effective. If yours isn't, stop.

In this section, I introduce a unique 8-step process that helps you to quickly create, validate, and communicate requirements that prepare you for action—in days, not weeks or months.

CHAPTER 11
BUILDING REQUIREMENTS FOR QUICK WINS AND BEYOND

 Poor requirements represent the top cause of troubled projects.[1]

- *PM Solutions Research*

CHAPTER 11

BUILDING REQUIREMENTS FOR QUICK WINS AND BEYOND

A lot's been written over the years about the subject of poor requirements. According to IBM, the inability to effectively understand user requirements is the leading cause of software failure.[2] The Standish Group says incomplete requirements represent the top reason organizations give for impaired projects.[3] And BusinessWeek Research Services ranks it among the top obstacles to avoid if you want to be successful with BI.[4]

Truth be told, creating requirements for business intelligence can be tough business. Not all decision-makers know what information they need to do their jobs, and pressure to drive performance in a constantly-changing business environment can make information requirements difficult to button-down. To make matters worse, most of the techniques used to gather requirements today are still systems- and software-oriented, and they are simply inadequate in delivering on the promise of BI with the speed and responsiveness required by today's business leaders. That is, until now.

The Quick Wins Model is an accelerated approach to creating, validating, and communicating requirements for BI. Its purpose is to help you deliver a comprehensive, business-aligned BI capability over time, one fast-paced step at a time. The 8-step process defines specific methods that help you work in fast, iterative cycles with a cross-functional group of stakeholders to identify high-value, low-risk areas of pressing business pain and the information required to eliminate it. Each of these resulting "quick wins" represents an opportunity for leaders to make an impact on the business within the next 90 days. The upfront preparation required by the model helps to ensure the alignment of each quick win so that you can effectively build an integrated, cohesive solution over time.

Painting the Big Picture
The Method: Aspirational Modeling
Covered in Chapter 12

Prioritizing Mission-Critical Information Needs
The Method: Key Question Analysis
Covered in Chapter 13

Defining the Information Universe
The Method: Information Modeling
Covered in Chapter 14

Validating the Information Model

The Method: Report Decomposition

Covered in Chapter 15

Bridging the Gap Between Business and IT

The Method: Model Transformation

Covered in Chapter 16

Mapping the Data

The Method: Source Data Analysis

Covered in Chapter 17

Creating the Execution Plan

The Method: Action Planning

Covered in Chapter 18

Documenting the Findings

The Method: Harmonization

Covered in Chapter 19

The process begins with a stakeholder workshop that uses "guided brainstorming" to elicit requirements. I say "guided" because the objective of the workshop isn't to generate a large number of ideas or concepts that result from traditional brainstorming. Rather, its purpose is to generate requirements from "front of mind" awareness associated with relevant topics guided by the workshop facilitator. The methods used (Step 1-3) provide a quick and effective way to gather stakeholder perspectives around prioritized quick wins and to define the supporting information universe you need to deliver on them.

Following the requirements-gathering workshop is a series of business analysis steps (Steps 4-8) that ultimately lead to a document of findings and a defined action plan. Individual interviews are reserved for any follow-up questions that might arise and to clarify any ambiguity.

One of the keys to maximizing the effectiveness of your work effort is ensuring you have a strong, foundational understanding of how your organization competes and makes money. In preparation for the workshop, take time to understand your firm's strategies and corporate initiatives, objectives, and departmental plans so that you can effectively guide stakeholder discussion.

One of the unique things about the Quick Wins Model is its focus on uncovering stakeholder expectations. Most of the time, getting a business user's view on important topics like people, processes, technology, and data is something that is either neglected entirely during traditional requirements-gathering exercises or simply overshadowed by a preoccupation with functional specifications. With the Quick Wins Model, it's a core activity. That's because understanding and effectively managing stakeholder expectations has a direct, significant, and lasting impact on solution adoption. Adoption is "personal buy-in"—a user's response to feeling involved, heard, and understood. In my experience, adoption issues are common with BI; they typically result, not from a lack of user need or interest, but from requirements that fail to adequately capture, create, validate, and communicate their expectations. At the end of the day, the level of adoption represents a real and practical way stakeholders tell us that their BI capability is in or out of alignment with their needs. By capturing expectations, you get valuable insight into emotions that can help propel a project to success or simply render it useless.

Using The Quick Wins Model, expect to complete the requirements workshop in as little as a ½ day. The amount of time it takes to finish related business analysis is largely dependent on the availability of accurate and detailed documentation. However, you should strive to wrap-up the entire process in under a week.

In the chapters that follow I provide a detailed explanation and guidelines for implementing each step in the process.

CHAPTER 12
PAINTING THE BIG PICTURE

" Strategic thinking does not deal with future decisions. It deals with the futurity of present decisions.[1] "

- *Peter F. Drucker*

PAINTING THE BIG PICTURE

Alvin Toffler, the American writer and futurist recognized by Accenture as one of the world's top business thought leaders, writes about the concept of "big picture" thinking. "You've got to think about big things while you are doing small things," says Toffler, "so that all of the small things go in the right direction."[2] That's particularly true in the world of business intelligence where decision-makers increasingly seek tactical solutions to help eliminate pressing business pain. It's a reflection of the demanding, fast-paced business climate in which most organizations operate—one that pressures stakeholders to create value as quickly as possible because decision-windows continue to shrink.[3]

Thing is, it takes diligence and an appropriate strategy to effectively integrate these tactical solutions into a coordinated and unified business intelligence capability. Those that fail to adequately plan ultimately pay the price with costly and uncoordinated information silos. Gartner analyst Betsy Burton predicts that companies without a cohesive BI strategy spend upwards of 70% of their total BI budget resolving issues around people, process, and technology that result from poor planning.[4]

"Painting the big picture" is the cornerstone of an effective and sustainable business intelligence competency and the first step in your requirements-gathering effort. "Big picture thinking," as Toffler puts it, is all about preparation. Thinking strategically helps you to adequately prepare before you deliver so that your work effort has future life.

With The Quick Wins Model, thinking strategically helps you to uncover and manage what I refer to as each firm's "strategic requirements"—non-functional requirements associated with 1) today's business environment; and 2) stakeholder expectations about how the environment should look tomorrow. The method I use to gather these requirements is called Aspirational Modeling.

Method   Aspirational Modeling

Purpose   To capture from key stakeholders
                        the current state of business, the
                        drivers behind BI, and top-of-mind
                        expectations around future-state
                        capabilities.

Expected Duration   60-120 minutes

Aspirational Modeling is a group brainstorming technique typically conducted with a cross-functional team of key business stakeholders and representatives of IT.

Lasting anywhere from 1 to 2 hours, its purpose is to capture strategic requirements that are "top of mind" for session participants (responses that simply roll off the tongue). When participants have to start thinking too much, the session ends. The output from this session provides invaluable insight into a business environment that, if left unattended, could negatively impact your execution plan. It also creates important awareness that empowers you to effectively manage and control stakeholder expectations.

The reference model (Figure 5) is something you can draw in front of your audience while you explain its significance. If you prefer, distribute it as a session handout. The purpose of the illustration is to spur critical thinking around topics relevant to strategic requirements-gathering, It is based on the idea that you can only help an organization achieve its aspirational or future state by first gaining an appreciation for 1) the firm's current operating environment; and 2) stakeholder expectations associated with people, process, technology, and data.

Each component of the reference model is described in the table on pages 76 and 77 including suggested questions to kick-start your brainstorming session.

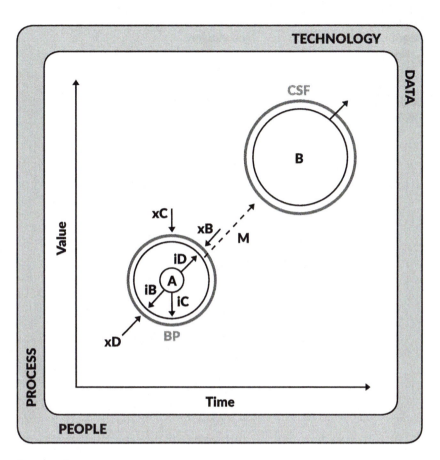

Legend

A	Point A	**iD**	Internal Drivers
B	Point B	**xD**	External Drivers
xC	External Constraints	**BP**	Big Plans
iB	Internal Barriers to Success	**CSF**	Critical Success Factors
xB	External Barriers to Success	**M**	Movement
iC	Internal Constraints		

Figure 5 – Aspirational Model

Strategic Requirements Category	Topic	Description
Business Environment	Point A	A quantifiable depiction of the organization's current state
	Point B	A quantifiable depiction of the organization's future state
	Movement (M)	The process of value-creation; typically reflected in one or more action verbs, identifies how stakeholders intend to move the organization from point A to point B
	Drivers (iD and xD)	The primary business motivators (also referred to as "business pain") propelling your BI initiative forward; can be internal pressure or external market forces
	Big Plans (BP)	Organization-wide initiatives (either planned or underway) that could impact your BI strategy and implementation roadmap if left unidentified. Applicable timeframe is 1 to 3 years
Stakeholder Expectations	Critical Success Factors (CSF)	Defines future-state "must haves" necessary for success
	Barriers to Succes (iB and xB)	Internal and/or external roadblocks that must be eliminated in order to be successful
	Constraints (iC and xC)	Known limitations that must be accommodated in order to be successful; can be internal and/or external

Questions to Get Things Started

How would you define, in measurable terms, where your company is today?

What's the goal? What will the current-state measures look like when you achieve your future-state vision?

How will you achieve your aspirational state?

What is driving your need for better access to information?

Within the next 3 years, what "big plans" associated with people, process, technology, or data are either in-flight or planned?

What future-state elements of people, process, technology, and data must exist for you to stand-up and say the work effort behind this BI initiative was an undeniable success?

What internal or external roadblocks associated with people, process, technology, or data must be knocked down and pushed out of the way in order for you to achieve the aspirational state?

What internal or external constraints around people, process, technology, or data must be accommodated in order for you to be successful?

Central to the concept of Aspirational Modeling is the expectation that actionable intelligence will help move the organization from its current state (point A) to a more valuable future state (point B). So, one of the critical pieces of information you need to capture and document from this session is the definition of value and a depiction of expected quantifiable business outcomes. It's the only way you can proactively monitor and evaluate BI performance against expectation and adhere to the Qualify Imperative I cover in Section 2.

Finally, it's always a good idea to close-out this step in the process by facilitating some "blue sky" thinking. Merriam-Webster defines the term as "visionary" thinking—"not grounded in the reality of the present."[5] It gives session participants the freedom to communicate ideas and concepts that didn't fit into earlier discussion, and it provides you with an opportunity to capture additional insight into potential future-state capabilities around people, process, technology, or data. Consider the ideas while you plan development and delivery, and you just may uncover a way to unexpectedly "wow" your internal customers. There's no better way to build momentum, excitement, and goodwill with the business than to pleasantly surprise your constituents by over-delivering. Simply approach "blue sky" thinking by asking a guided question like, "If you had a magic wand and no barriers or no constraints, what would your business intelligence capability look like?"

_____

The information you capture in this session you'll use to inform and influence the development and implementation of the Execution Plan I discuss in Chapter 18.

Now that you have a picture of the business environment and are aware of important stakeholder expectations, you're ready for Step 2.

CHAPTER 13
PRIORITIZING MISSION-CRITICAL INFORMATION NEEDS

> *A majority of business decision makers don't have ready access to high-quality, reliable, useful information on operating and financial performance at their companies.[1]*

- Randy Myers

PRIORITIZING MISSION-CRITICAL INFORMATION NEEDS

Your ability to deliver insight that's relevant, timely, and actionable requires a fundamental understanding of the key strategic, tactical, and operational questions decision-makers attempt to answer on a routine basis. In Chapter 6, I discussed the Unifying Principle that "not all data matters." Well, not all questions matter either—at least when it comes to establishing priorities around the delivery of a business intelligence capability.

The expected outcome of this step in the process is the identification of "mission-critical" business questions. Mission-critical questions are those that keep your business stakeholders up at night—the first questions they ask when they arrive at work and the last questions they ask before they leave.

Method   Key Question Analysis

Purpose   To identify and prioritize top-of-mind,
                    mission-critical business questions
                    (also called "key questions") and the
                    expected outcomes to answering them

Expected Duration   60-120 minutes

With this method, the questions you capture provide you with important visibility into the world decision-makers are trying to manage right now. You will use this documented insight in three important ways:

1) To validate the content of the Information Universe you'll create in the next step of the requirements-gathering process
2) To ensure the self-service reporting and analytics capability you design and deliver in the near-term supports the prioritized needs of your stakeholders
3) To monitor expected business outcomes

I often jumpstart this guided brainstorming session by asking: "As business leaders, you're going to lose your job if you can't answer what business questions?" I like to establish "job loss" as a consequence because it naturally raises the level of importance in the mind of session participants.

I also purposely limit discussion to what I believe is a manageable list of top-of-mind responses, like the top three.

Keep in mind that most initial responses are pretty vague. A vague question is one that can't easily be answered without first answering one or more underlying root questions. So use your role as facilitator to help stakeholders uncover clear and unambiguous key questions.

Consider this simple real-world example from an interaction I had with a sales executive:

He phrased one of his initial key questions like this: "Who is my best sales representative?" It's a vague question because the adjective "best" is undefined. I first got him to restate the question into a version that defines "best" in order to eliminate the ambiguity. The result was, "Which sales representative generates the most margin?" With one more iteration, he created an even better version with greater specificity: "Which sales representative generates the most margin by month." He then went on to define margin as revenue minus cost. You get the point.

Next, challenge stakeholders to identify the specific business outcome, value, or impact associated with answering each individual question. Ask them, "How will answering the question enable you to sell more, spend less, or work smarter?" Outcomes can be quantitative—meaning they are measurable; or qualitative—meaning they provide some important capability that empowers more effective decision-making. If you find a stakeholder struggling to identify expected business outcomes, it could be an indication that the question isn't as important as he or she thinks.

In Step 3 you'll work with stakeholders to graphically depict the universe of the information required to answer mission-critical business questions. Creating seed content for this exercise is helpful to building momentum. Do this by picking one or two questions that generated a lot of emotional response from session participants and decompose them into two distinct parts:

1) The "business measure" represented by the quantitative value
2) The "business dimension" or qualitative information that gives each measure context

I recommend that you circle each measure and underline each dimension for quick reference. Here's an illustration of how to break down the sales executive's question:

Which sales representative generates the most margin by month?

A couple of points to keep in mind:
- A dimension is always a noun
- A dimension will always follow the preposition "by"

However, depending on how a question is phrased, you may find a dimension depicted as an adjective as illustrated in this example:

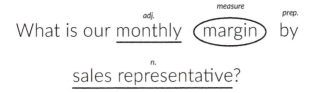

Once you break-down your seed questions into their component parts, you're ready for Step 3.

CHAPTER 14
BUILDING THE INFORMATION UNIVERSE

 Multidimensional managers are the new unit of competitive advantage.[1]

- The Multidimensional Manager: 24 Ways to Impact Your Bottom Line in 90 Days

BUILDING THE INFORMATION UNIVERSE

The Information Universe is a logical representation of the information decision-makers need to effectively monitor and measure the business. It documents in a business-centric, graphical form quantitative values like revenue (called business measures) and their relationship to qualitative information like month and sales representative (called business dimensions). A business dimension brings context to one or more otherwise meaningless measures by answering the "who, what, when, where, and how" of business performance. The resulting illustration, depicted in Figure 6, is known colloquially as a "Spider Diagram."

Method	Information Modeling
Purpose	To graphically-depict the stakeholder-defined "universe of information" required to effectively answer mission-critical business questions.
Expected Duration	90-120 minutes

This method represents an important advancement in requirements-definition for BI because it works the way decision-makers think. In their book, *The Multidimensional Manager: 24 Ways to Impact Your Bottom Line in 90 Days*, authors Richard Connelly, Robin McNeill, and Roland Mosimann write that "Managers think multidimensionally"—meaning they naturally and often simultaneously consider multiple variables or "dimensions" of the business when evaluating performance through measures.[2] The authors add, "To accelerate their understanding of the business, managers need to receive information in a format that matches the way they think." Makes sense, then, that we use a requirements-gathering method that enables decision-makers to provide information requirements the way they think, too.[3]

Typical requirements elicitation methods rely on business leaders to identify specific data they need or define the reports they want. Not so with information modeling. This method is a business discussion focused on how the organization operates through the lens of information.

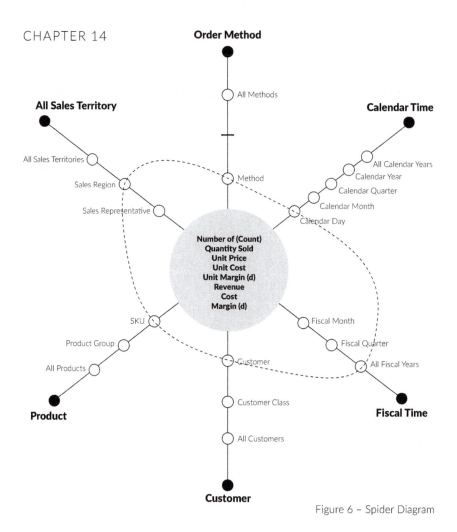

Figure 6 – Spider Diagram

The real benefit of the resulting Spider Diagram is the way it documents any potential "measure-dimension" combination without requiring business users to explicitly define them. Its power becomes evident when you "connect the dots" to uncover a virtually limitless combination of questions business leaders can ask of a self-service analytics capability—without the prerequisite of defining those questions upfront.

This business-focused diagram is ultimately used during solution design to bridge the Understanding Gap discussed in Chapter 10—that all too common disconnect between the needs communicated by business and those interpreted by IT.

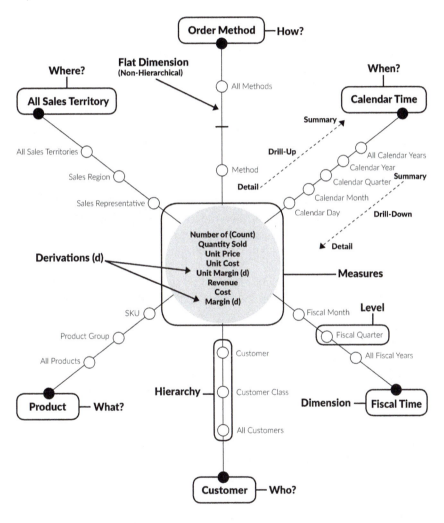

Figure 7– Components of the Spider Diagram

Term	Definition
Measure	A fact. A number or quantity that records a directly observable value or performance.[4]
Derivation	A derived measure or calculation; identified by the notation (d).
Dimension	A collection of reference information about a measurable event or fact. Dimensions categorize and describe data warehouse facts and measures in ways that support meaningful answers to business questions.[5]
Drill-Down	Means "give me more detail";[6] the process of navigating a dimension from summary information to more detailed information.
Drill-Up	Means "give me less detail"; the process of navigating a dimension from detailed information to summary information.
Flat Dimension	A dimension with a single level; a non-hierarchical dimension.
Hierarchy	A tree-like organizational structure used to relate values of a dimension to measures. Hierarchies enable the quantitative data associated with dimension values to be aggregated at various levels along the structure.[7]
Level	A position within a dimension hierarchy.[8]

Begin this requirements-gathering discussion by educating your audience on the process of information modeling. Take a minute to explain measures by referencing the quantitative values you identified and circled in Step 2. Then introduce the topic of dimensions. I like to use "time" (both calendar and fiscal) and the various levels that typically make it up as an example of a hierarchical dimension. You can use "order method" as an easy-to-understand example of a flat or non-hierarchical dimension that represents a single, mutually-exclusive selection between two or more possible choices (ex. internet or store).

To build the required momentum you need in an information modeling session, I recommend you start facilitation around the topic of measures. Seed a new measures list by pulling the values you documented during the Key Question Analysis. That way, you can illustrate to your stakeholders the important link between their most important business questions and the underlying Information Universe that supports answering them. Follow-up with a statement similar to, "Now tell me the other quantitative values you need to see on a regular basis to effectively monitor and measure your business." You'll know it's time to move on to dimensions when participants start struggling to identify measures they really care about.

To get the audience focused on dimensions, I find it helpful to reiterate to them the point that measures, without context, are meaningless. It's only when decision-makers look at measures "by something" that the quantitative values provide insight into performance. Each "by something" represents a dimension of the business. Getting stakeholders to think in those terms is an effective way of identifying and documenting all of the dimensions relevant to their business. Again, go back to the results of your Key Question Analysis. Reference the dimensions (represented by the nouns and adjectives) as a starting point for creating the Spider Diagram.

Remember that the objective of a business modeling session is to produce a Spider Diagram like the one presented earlier in this chapter, only customized to the unique needs of your stakeholders. You do this by facilitating a business-centric rather than a data-centric brainstorming session. At no time should you discuss the availability, accessibility, quality, or mapping of data.

Now it's time to validate the model.

CHAPTER 15
VALIDATING THE INFORMATION MODEL

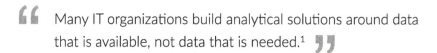 Many IT organizations build analytical solutions around data that is available, not data that is needed.[1]

- CFO Insights

VALIDATING THE INFORMATION MODEL

Report Decomposition is a requirements validation technique used to ensure the information universe you created is as accurate and complete as possible. It works by comparing future-state information requirements reflected in the Spider Diagram with content from mission-critical reports currently in use by business stakeholders.

Method   Report Decomposition

Purpose   To ensure the accuracy and
                        completeness of the information model
                        by comparing it to content from
                        mission-critical reports currently in use.

Expected Duration   60-180 minutes

Report decomposition is a relatively simple process that begins with securing the Top three mission-critical reports from each of your business stakeholders. A mission-critical report is any document, printed or electronic, that contains information the decision-maker simply "can't live without." Three reports is an arbitrary but practical number I use to limit the scope of analysis.

The process requires you to "decompose" each report into its component parts: quantitative values (like dollar amounts) and qualitative or descriptive information (like dates, customers, and products). You do this by evaluating column headings, underlying data formats, and content that appears in report headers and footers. Note any calculated measures along with their associated formulas.

Now compare your documented list of report components to your Spider Diagram. Quantitative values should map to measures, and qualitative information should map to a level of a dimension. You should never find information on a mission critical report that isn't reflected in the Spider Diagram. If you do, update the Spider Diagram accordingly.

Another part of the validation step is to create a reference table (called an Information Validation Matrix) that identifies the measures and dimensions required to answer each of the key questions from your analysis in Step #2.

The work product should look something like the illustration that follows but contain all of the measures and dimensions depicted in your Spider Diagram.

Information Model Validation Matrix

Measure	Dimension	Dimension Level	Key Questions
			Which sales representative generates the most margin by month?
Revenue			x
Cost			x
Margin			d
	Calendar Time	Year	
		Quarter	
		Month	x
		Day	
	Sales Territory	Sales Region	
		Sales Representative	x

Whenever possible, I prefer to keep measures and dimensions together in the same matrix. In fact, you'll notice that I use this same format when we tackle data mapping in Chapter 17.

However, format the crosstab in a way that best suits your needs. Depending on the number of key questions, measures, and dimensions, you may decide to change the orientation or to place measures and dimensions in separate tables.

CHAPTER 16
BRIDGING THE GAP BETWEEN BUSINESS AND IT

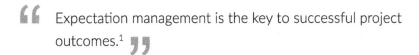 Expectation management is the key to successful project outcomes.[1]

- *Jeff Gainer*

BRIDGING THE GAP BETWEEN BUSINESS AND IT

Every day some very smart and well-intentioned people attempt to get business and IT to see eye-to-eye, too often with mediocre results. One part of the problem is cultural and, as I discussed in Chapter 10, can only be addressed through effective collaboration. The other part of the problem is the inherent disconnect between the way business and technology professionals view and discuss the worlds they live in.

The Spider Diagram is an effective technique for eliciting and documenting information requirements because it mimics the way business users think. Its format, though, does very little to foster understanding for practitioners in IT responsible for specifying, building, and delivering on those needs. That's where Model Transformation comes in.

Method   Model Transformation

Purpose   To help align business and IT by
                       transforming the business-defined
                       information model into a form and
                       format technologists understand.

Expected Duration   120-140 minutes

Model Transformation bridges The Understanding Gap (see Figure 4 in Chapter 10) by quickly and easily transforming the Spider Diagram into a form and language technologists readily understand: the star schema.

Oracle's Data Warehousing Guide describes the star schema this way:

"The star schema is the simplest data warehouse schema. It is called a star schema because the diagram of a star schema resembles a star, with points radiating from a center. The center of the star consists of a fact table and the points of the star are the dimension tables."[2]

Dimension tables are lookup tables. They contain primary keys and related categorical information associated with the dimension hierarchy. The fact table consists of business measures and the relevant keys that link those measures to each dimension.

Figure 8 depicts the output of the Model Transformation process using the Spider Diagram from Chapter 14.

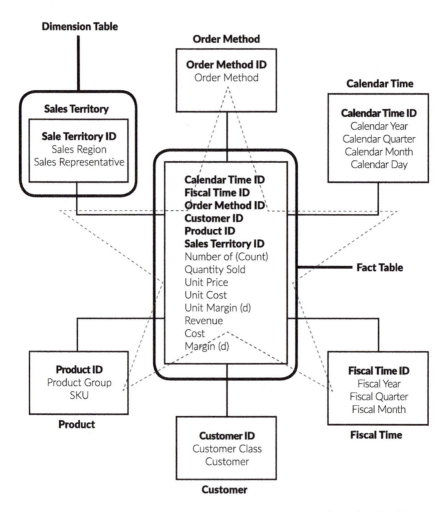

Figure 8 – Star Schema

To transform a Spider Diagram into a star schema like the one in Figure 8, follow these 5 steps:

1) Create a star schema fact table by replicating all of the quantitative values contained in your Spider Diagram measures list

2) Create a star schema dimension table for each dimension from the Spider Diagram

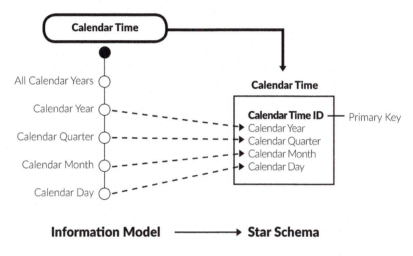

Figure 9 - Dimension Replication

3) Within each star schema dimension table, replicate the dimension levels depicted in the Spider Diagram

4) For each star schema dimension, create a generic dimension ID and place it at the top of the attribute list. This represents the dimension's primary key

5) Copy each dimension ID and place at the top of the fact table measures list. These represent the fact table foreign keys

Now you have a tool to effectively communicate information requirements in a form technologists understand.

While many organizations physically implement star schema data structures to support reporting and analytics requirements, I reference it here only in a logical sense as a way to effectively communicate. Your team of information architects is best-suited to make appropriate data warehouse design decisions based on the myriad of factors they need to consider beyond just information requirements.

CHAPTER 17
MAPPING THE DATA

" Business does not work through features and functions, but through processes. Business requirements need to be defined in business process terms—how the organization wants to do business, compete and make money in the future.[1] "

- Jed Simms

MAPPING THE DATA

Now that you've identified the information decision-makers need to do their jobs and have documented it in a form and format that both the business and IT understand, it's time to identify relevant data sources to populate the facts and dimensions of your model. This is where the real work begins.

Take a quick scan through just about any book on business intelligence or data warehousing and you uncover what appears to be the norm for most organizations—a tidy, orderly flow of information from various data sources to a data warehouse where it is staged for end-user reporting and analysis.[2] In my experience, that's simply not the case. Well-documented data sources and process flows represent the exception, not the rule.

Method	Source Data Analysis
Purpose	To locate required source data and identify the extent to which it is available, accessible, and adequate.
Expected Duration	1-3 days

In their book, *The Profit Impact of Business Intelligence,* authors Steve and Nancy Williams write about the challenge of data sources and the purpose of effective requirements-gathering. "Business needs the information it needs," they write, "regardless of whether there is a currently available source for that information."[3] In the preceding chapters, I cover logical representations of information your decision-makers need to monitor and measure the business. In this step of the Quick Wins Method, our attention turns to Source Data Analysis in order to understand the extent to which you can satisfy the information needs of your business stakeholders.

In Chapter 15, I describe Report Decomposition as a requirements validation technique used to ensure the information model defined by your stakeholders reflects all of the content they use day-in and day-out from their mission-critical reports. The Information Model Validation Matrix is then used to identify specific measures and dimensions necessary to answer each of the stakeholders' key questions. We'll use that matrix as a starting point for Source Data Analysis.

The purpose of Source Data Analysis is to help you answer three important questions relating to the measures and dimensions depicted in the Information Model Validation Matrix:

1) Is the data available? (i.e. Does it exist in the form and format you need? If not, can it be derived?)

2) Is the data accessible? (i.e. Do you have authority to access it, or do security and/or regulatory restrictions prevent access or use?)

3) Is the data quality good enough? (i.e. Is the data reliable enough to make required business decisions?)

Source Data Analysis is, arguably, the most important step in delivering quick wins. It requires a strong, collaborative effort between business and IT, and those participating in the process have to be willing to think creatively about data.

Start by creating a simple Data Mapping Table like the one depicted on the following page (Figure 10). For simplicity's sake, I like to use the information model Validation Matrix as my primary reference document for tying together my key questions, the information model, and data mappings. Doing so helps me to quickly uncover gaps in my analysis, discover issues that require attention, and to expose key questions that can't be supported by data.

Work with data domain experts to complete the table by identifying the appropriate source mappings and addressing data access and quality concerns. Use the columns associated with data access and data quality to indicate yes or no.

Measure	Dimension	Dimension Level	Is the data available?			Is the data accessible?	Is the data quality good enough?
			Source System	Source Table	Source Attribute		
Revenue							
Cost							
Margin							
	Calendar Time	Calendar Year					
		Calendar Quarter					
		Calendar Month					
		Calendar Day					
	Sales Territory	Sales Region					
		Sales Representative					

Notes

1	
2	
3	

Figure 10 – Data Mapping Table

When necessary, provide a reference number that links to the notes section of the table where you can adequately explain issues, concerns, and thoughts on risk mitigation. Be sure to identify any source data granularity issues that could impact data integration.

Keep in mind that locating appropriate data may not be as simple as tapping an existing data mart or data warehouse. It might mean integrating it from multiple standalone spreadsheets located throughout the organization or going back to transactional systems.

One of the tools I find useful in helping to identify and map source transaction data is a type of data flow diagram I created based on the Michael Porter's Value Chain Framework.[4] I call it the Information Supply Chain—a generic model you can customize to the needs of your specific business (Figure 11).

The model uses action verbs to depict the various value-creating and interrelated activities associated with Porter's framework. You can use it to graphically depict the creation and movement of data from system to system throughout your information supply chain. You can even overlay platforms, databases, attributes, and timing of data movement.

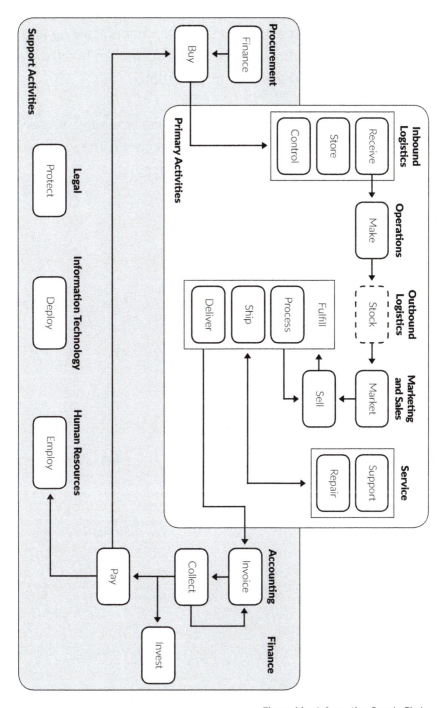

Figure 11 – Information Supply Chain

I've used it to map the life of an order in manufacturing and, with some modifications, the life of a patient in healthcare and the life of a package in transportation.

The objective is to identify where the data you need actually lives, and to do it quickly. Use whatever tool is relevant and at your disposal to achieve your objective.

CHAPTER 18
CREATING THE EXECUTION PLAN

" For all the talk of Big Data, Mobile BI, Predictive Analytics and Data Visualization, the evidence is that the real management information needs of most executives are far more down-to-earth: fast, easy, self-service access to data—for the people that need it, and from whichever data sources are relevant.[1] "

- Matthew Scullion

CREATING THE EXECUTION PLAN

To prepare for accelerated execution, it's important to distill all of the requirements you've captured into a strategically-aligned execution plan you can deliver with a high-probability of success. You'll use this plan to guide development activity and to establish and manage stakeholder expectations around the phased implementation of prioritized quick wins. Consider it your "quick wins roadmap."

Method	Action Planning
Purpose	To prepare for accelerated execution by distilling mission-critical information requirements into a risk-mitigated action plan.
Expected Duration	1-3 days

The method I use to build recommendations is a process called Action Planning. As Figure 12 illustrates, the Input-Evaluate-Recommend Model displays the artifacts you use and the key questions you ask in order to establish the risk-mitigated execution plan.

Turn to your notes from the Aspirational Modeling exercise for the input you need into your organization's vision. The findings you documented from the requirements-gathering workshop and related business analysis work provides the input associated with quick wins.

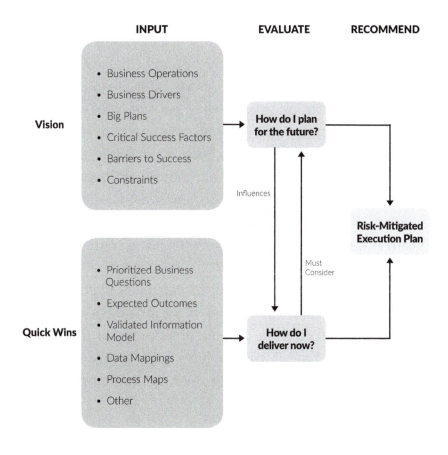

Figure 12 – Input-Evaluate-Recommend Model

117

Your objective is to create a risk-mitigated execution plan that accomplishes three things:

1) Delivers your prioritized quick wins (fast!)
2) Maximizes re-use of the information assets
3) Future-proofs your work effort

The first and primary objective of your execution plan is to deliver the prioritized quick wins and to do it as fast as possible.

As you consider quick wins, give thought to how you can maximize the re-use of your work effort, especially the resulting information assets. It's one of the important ways you can continually improve the speed at which you deliver value to the business. Each quick win builds upon and leverages the other, so you should see over time: a) a natural evolution of your information model—that is, the addition of new measures and dimensions to support new business questions; and b) data overlap—the commonality of existing measures and dimensions shared between business units and stakeholders. As your BI capability matures, data overlap will become more and more prevalent, and you will see it reflected in re-usable components of the Spider Diagram. Over time it will evolve into a complete logical representation of your organization's information needs around decision support.

Future-proofing is all about minimizing rework. I say "minimize" because it's impossible to eliminate it. People, processes, technology, and data are in a perpetual state of evolution. However, you can help create long-lasting value by answering this question: "How do I effectively plan for the future?" Allow all of the vision-related inputs to inform your thinking, and have a strategy for addressing the people, process, technology, and data components of each. What critical success factors do you plan on supporting and when? If your firm is in the process of sunsetting a system that provides important data necessary for a quick win, how will you handle that? How do you plan on knocking down people barriers or process constraints that could impact your ability to be successful?

With the knowledge you captured during your requirements-gathering session and analysis work, the execution plan formalizes your recommendation for delivering a BI capability that accelerates value. The roadmap will naturally evolve over time as you work with different line of business stakeholders who communicate new quick win opportunities.

As a part of building your action plan, be sure to document key decisions, design considerations, and dependencies. It's always helpful to include a question and answer section, too.

CHAPTER 19
DOCUMENTING YOUR FINDINGS

" When it comes to thorough, well-written documentation, there are no shortcuts. "

DOCUMENTING YOUR FINDINGS

The final step of the Quick Wins Model is the creation of a complete and thorough findings and recommendations document. It is the primary vehicle you use to cement stakeholder commitment and to educate and inform those business and IT professionals who didn't participate in the requirements-gathering process. A well-designed and well-written requirements document is a must-have.

Method	Harmonization
Purpose	To align and harmonize the organization's understanding of information requirements by documenting your findings in an easy-to-digest form
Expected Duration	1-3 days

The clarity that comes with effective documentation helps eliminate misunderstanding and, as a result, drives cooperation and teamwork needed for BI success. All of the content you need to create this work product was captured over the course of the quick wins process. Now, follow these tips to create a findings document that helps to align and harmonize your organization.

Align and Harmonize Tip #1 – Embrace the opportunity

Most practitioners consider documentation a nuisance—a tedious and unappreciated task. That's one of the reasons why most documentation (when it even exists!) is incomplete and carelessly written. Approach documentation with a different mindset. Consider the creation of thorough, complete, and well-written documentation a responsibility you owe your stakeholders and an opportunity you owe yourself. You should take it personally because the quality of this high-profile document ultimately reflects on you.

Align and Harmonize Tip #2 – Use visual aids

Most people benefit from visual aids, especially when it comes to understanding the complexities associated with defining and delivering technology-based solutions. So, to the extent you can, enhance your findings and recommendations document with relevant pictures, diagrams, illustrations, and examples to help eliminate ambiguity and avoid misunderstanding.

Align and Harmonize Tip #3 – Elaborate

When preparing your findings and recommendation document, assume your audience knows very little about BI or your initiative. It will force you to provide important background material and relevant context in order to effectively educate and inform. Avoid jargon and, instead, use plain English. As a practice, communicate more than you feel is necessary.

Align and Harmonize Tip #4 – Document everything

I'm a proponent of documenting everything you discover before, during, and after your requirements-gathering and analysis efforts. Whatever it is, get it out of your head and onto paper. The more you and your colleagues know, the better you can plan and execute. And when it comes to creating your findings and recommendations document, don't wing it. Start with a well-organized, comprehensive, and logical structure like the one presented below, then customize it to suit your specific needs. By the way, create your documentation along the way. Putting it off until later only creates anxiety, and you risk forgetting important nuances that could impact an adequate understanding of need.

Sample Table of Contents for Findings and Recommendations Document

Revision Record

Stakeholder Participant List

Stakeholder Signoff Matrix

Section 1.0 – Overview

Section 1.1 – The Requirements-Gathering Process

Section 1.2 – Purpose

Section 1.3 – Scope

Section 1.4 – Objectives

Section 1.5 – Assumptions

Section 2.0 – Findings

Section 2.1 – Terminology and Business Definitions

Section 2.2 – Business Operations

Section 2.3 – Business Drivers

Section 2.4 – Big Plans

Section 2.5 – Critical Success Factors

Section 2.6 – Barriers to Success

Section 2.7 – Constraints

Section 2.8 – Prioritized Business Questions

Section 2.9 – Expected Outcomes

Section 2.10 – Information Model

Section 2.11 – Data Mappings

Section 2.12 – Process Maps

Section 2.13 – User Community

Section 2.14 – Security

Section 2.15 – Governance

Section 2.16 – References and Key Documents

Section 3.0 – Recommendations

Section 3.1 – Execution Plan

Section 3.2 – Key Decisions

Section 3.3 – Design Considerations and Dependencies

Section 3.4 – Questions and Answers

Section 3.5 – Conclusion

Appendix – Supporting Documentation

Align and Harmonize Tip #5 – Set aggressive priorities for review and feedback

If you're going to make movement on quick wins, you have to set aggressive priorities for the review, feedback, and signoff on your findings and recommendations document. Before you wrap-up your requirements workshop, be clear with stakeholders about your expectations. In the same way you gathered requirements as a group, I always recommend a formal presentation of finding and recommendations to the group as well. Set the tentative date before you leave the room, and make sure everyone knows that signoff or "signoff with agreed-upon changes" will occur at that session. In the meantime, stay in touch with stakeholders and keep them updated on your progress.

SECTION 4
WAYS TO ACCELERATE EXECUTION

With requirements in hand and your quick wins roadmap in place, it's time to turn your attention to execution. Just remember, "BI is not for the faint of heart."[1] Each cycle needs to be fast, it needs to be visible, and it has to evolve.

In this section, I cover 3 important topics that are vital to ensuring your execution goes off without a hitch: speed, promotion, and continuous improvement. I've included a reference model, too, that helps tie it all together for you.

CHAPTER 20
BE QUICK AND NIMBLE

❝ Dinosaurs must learn to become pumas.[1] ❞

- *Tom Clive*

BE QUICK AND NIMBLE

In business today, it is imperative that organizations find a way to capitalize on opportunities that surface from market disruption. In fact, "...a fiercely competitive business environment [has] led 'agility' to trump 'perfectly architected'"[2] when it comes to building a business intelligence capability that effectively supports decision-making. And rightfully so. Organizations have to be quick and nimble. They need to be empowered to make smart and timely business decisions based on real-world dynamics.[3]

Follow these tips to ensure that you are operating in a quick and nimble fashion.

Quick and Nimble Tip #1 - Embrace agile principles

Familiarize yourself with The Twelve Principles of Agile Software[4] and make the concepts a part of the way you think. They were established to satisfy the customer through early and continuous delivery of valuable software, and the principles reflect many of the same philosophies espoused in this book. Always remember that "agility is driven by the need to serve end users. It's about always being relevant and responsive."[5]

Quick and Nimble Tip #2 - Build quick win pilots

Today, the primary focus of BI is the delivery of self-service interactive dashboards for at-a-glance business monitoring, management-by-exception, and analytics. A process I call "fast piloting"—meaning the creation of representative information dashboards in hours or days, not weeks—is a great way to 1) visually validate requirements while they're still fresh in the minds of your business stakeholders; and 2) deliver real value. Know that some enterprise BI platforms can turn this process from fast to agonizingly slow and can, as a result, defeat its inherent purpose. Instead, consider the use of advanced data visualization products to make fast piloting a reality

Quick and Nimble Tip #3: Leverage operational reports for data extraction

Don't reinvent the wheel. Key operational reports can and often do provide the source content you need to build pilots that deliver real value. So, use them as your data extraction method. Run a report, save the data to a file, and read the output into an advanced data visualization tool.

Quick-and-Nimble Tip #4 - Under-promise, over-deliver

Did you know that many of the unreasonable expectations we find ourselves managing are the direct result of things we say or unintended impressions we leave? That's been my experience. When we overcommit, we set ourselves up for failure. And nothing frustrates business users more than when we tell them one thing but do another. "Under-promise, over-deliver" is a best practice for helping you deliver on-target, on-budget, on-time, every time.

Quick and Nimble Tip #5 - Over-communicate

Nobody likes surprises, so communicate more than necessary more often than necessary. It's a practice that goes a long way to building trust and cooperative partnerships with people. Utilize a project dashboard that quickly and concisely communicates relevant details of interest to stakeholders.

Quick and Nimble Tip #6 - Practice "controlled flexibility"

"Controlled flexibility" is an agile principle that allows for last-minute, business-critical changes to requirements that have minimal impact on schedule or cost. BI initiatives aren't well-suited to the traditional design-build-test-deploy cycle of application development—a process business users often find too rigid and constraining. Business users like to partner with practitioners who understand that it's "impossible to remember everything" and who are committed to ensuring requirements that were inadvertently missed are included, when reasonable and practical, in the delivered solution.

Quick and Nimble Tip #7 – Make lightweight governance an inseparable part of your effort

Governing data means effectively managing it: maintaining consistency, reducing redundancy, and ensuring its quality. But these days, attempting to implement data governance as a standalone initiative is often impractical. So, make it an inseparable part of your BI development effort to gain and maintain traction. The key is to keep it lightweight. The best place to start is the business glossary. Use it to engage and align key stakeholders around common data definitions, then expand from there. Just remember that data governance is evolutionary, not revolutionary. When it comes to getting started with data governance, the important thing is to get started.

Quick and Nimble Tip #8 – Use lightweight project management

Implement just the right amount of project management to ensure adequate visibility, transparency, and communication. When you start to spend more time worrying about satisfying the Project Management Office (PMO) than you do your business stakeholders, it's a good sign the project management requirements are too heavy. Use a simple and effective RAID log to capture and communicate Risks, Actions, Issues, and key Decisions. It's a great way to keep everyone involved on the same page.

Quick and Nimble Tip #9 - Prepare to scale

While quick wins are primarily meant to satisfy the tactical, short-term needs of decision-makers, they aren't throw-away. In fact, they can often provide long-lasting value. Whenever possible and pragmatic, prepare to operationalize and scale your quick win pilots by adhering to relevant design and development standards established by your enterprise architects and systems administrators.

Quick and Nimble Tip #10: Get organized

Your ability to be quick and nimble is tied to how well organized you are. Make sure you have the right tools at your disposal. Build a library of standard templates, scripts, and other artifacts you can reuse from one quick win effort to another so you don't waste valuable time. You can even create a sandbox to pre-stage data if it helps. Whatever works. The point is: get organized and stay that way.

CHAPTER 21
SOCIALIZE, MARKET AND SELL

" Avoid the negative impact of skeptics and naysayers by building excitement around your BI efforts. "

SOCIALIZE, MARKET AND SELL

Creating a data-driven culture requires more than the successful delivery of quick wins. It requires the alignment of an aware, knowledgeable, and engaged business community that works to transform business through more effective decision-making, and evangelism is critical to making that happen.

Consider yourself a business-oriented technology evangelist. Your job is to amplify (as I discuss in Chapter 8)—to socialize, market, and sell the vision and benefits of a business intelligence capability. You do this to educate, inform, and motivate your audience into a critical mass of support[1] that helps drive adoption and long-term sustainability.

To amplify means to raise your voice and be heard. Here are some tips for making that happen.

Amplify Tip #1 – Create an identity
When you create an identity for your BI initiative, you empower yourself to internally market and sell in ways that engage your audience. Think contests, events, posters, banners, T-shirts. And don't just name your initiative, brand it. "When you think about your brand," says *Forbes* contributing writer Lois Gellar, "think about all the elements [that make it up]: promise, personality, look, voice, service, attributes, memorability, even [impression]."[2]

A brand sets expectations around value and gives your stakeholders something to hold onto. Hey, if you want a best-in-class BI capability, act best-in-class.

Amplify Tip #2 – Establish advocates

Not everyone is a skeptic. Dedicate time to identifying advocates—those business and IT practitioners who "get BI" and can act as your surrogates in their circles of influence. Build rapport and invite them into your inner circle. Advocates are a great way to informally educate, to casually inform, and to spread key messages that are necessary for building the support you need for long-term success.

Amplify Tip #3 – Promote your successes

Nothing generates more buzz or builds more momentum than a great story. Promote the delivery of every quick win, and make sure your entire organization hears about the success stories from sales, marketing, finance, and operations that result from the use of BI. Excited people talk, so get people excited!

Amplify Tip #4 – Communicate often

Education and transparency are good things. So, think of simple and easy ways to routinely "over-communicate" key messages, status updates, project countdowns, and other information of interest to your audience. Use a newsletter, an intranet page, or strategically-placed posters. Give business unit leaders weekly talking points they can deliver during staff meetings. Or get creative and produce a series of podcasts or web videos on your success stories. You can even interview decision-makers from the set of your very own virtual studio.

Amplify Tip #5 – Be prepared for questions and feedback

Once you open-up broad-based communication with your audience, expect a lot of questions and considerable feedback. Consider it a prime opportunity to deepen the level of engagement. Be responsive and appreciative. In fact, consider publishing a running Q&A in your newsletter or highlighting feedback in your podcast to promote free-flowing discussion and idea generation.

CHAPTER 22
MONITOR, EVALUATE AND EVOLVE

 Continuous improvement is a key success factor for healthy BI implementations.[1]

- Boris Evelson

MONITOR, EVALUATE AND EVOLVE

Building a BI competency is an evolutionary process. That's one of the reasons I created the Quick Wins Model. It helps guide you through quick iterations of planning and execution cycles so that you have the opportunity to "fail fast." That's important because real learning happens and real insight results from trial and error. In their book, *The Wisdom of Failure: How to Learn the Tough Leadership Lessons Without Paying the Price*, authors Larry Weinzimmer and Jim McConoughey talk about the importance of failure on the road to success. "Failure is the only option," they write, "if success is the end goal."[2]

That's hard to hear if you work for one of the many organizations that have invested significant time and energy in BI and still struggle to see success. Sure, some deployments work and generate measurable results. But according to at least one prominent survey of BI users, "the majority [of BI deployments] are stuck in the middle, with respondents reporting only slight to moderate success and business impact."[3]

Unfortunately, organizations forget that business intelligence is a journey—a process of continuous improvement meant to adapt and evolve. As I pointed out in Chapter 9, many practitioners build and deliver a capability but then think the work is done. They don't take the time to qualify success, and few organizations proactively monitor and measure BI performance.

There are two important and related questions you need to ask yourself in order to effectively monitor, evaluate, and evolve your BI competency:

1) Is the information and analytic capability I'm providing helping to generate the business outcomes my stakeholders expect when they expect them?

2) Is my business intelligence environment high-performing?

Early in the quick wins process you asked those participating in the Aspirational Modeling session to answer this question: "What future-state elements of people, process, technology, and data must exist for you to stand-up and say the work effort behind this BI initiative was an undeniable success?" The result was a series of critical success factors—future-state "must haves" necessary for success. Remember, too, that you asked participants in the requirements workshop to formulate key questions that represent their top mission-critical information needs and to identify the business value in answering them. With these expectations in-hand, monitor and evaluate the performance of each quick win. Enhance those areas that are "on target" so you can drive even greater value. For those that are missing the mark, analyze why and then adjust accordingly. Remember that BI success "doesn't just happen." It is a process of continuous improvement.

The same holds true for your physical environment. A high-performing BI environment is one that is responsive to the needs of its user community. "BI performance efficiency and effectiveness metrics play a key role in improving the efficacy of the BI environment. Companies that track these metrics can contextualize BI usage patterns and trends to predict requests from users before they even make them."[4] Forrester Research calls this "BI on BI" and has established a body-of-knowledge on the subject.[5] Interestingly enough, only about half of BI pros take the time to quantitatively measure the effectiveness or efficiency of the environments they manage.[6] Like information access and analytic capability, creating a responsive environment is an evolutionary process. "Everyone collects statistics on the database and BI application server performance, and many [even] conduct periodic surveys to gauge business users' level of satisfaction," writes Boris Evelson. "But how do you really know if you have a high-performing, widely used, popular BI environment?"[7] Great question.

While BI on BI is largely unchartered territory[8] for many organizations, you can start by monitoring usage patterns of measures, dimensions, dashboards, and reports. Consider, too, the reasonableness of user-system interaction by measuring fundamental efficiency metrics like the "average number of clicks to find a report" or the "number of clicks within a report to find an answer to a question." Answers to questions like these should inform practical decisions around system improvements that will help solidify adoption.

CHAPTER 23
BRINGING IT ALL TOGETHER

> A reference model formalizes recommended practices and is a valuable tool in fostering understanding and guiding action.

BRINGING IT ALL TOGETHER

This book presents a number of methods and tips to help you accelerate the planning and execution of a BI competency. I developed the Hyper Framework (Figure 13) to help you visually organize these elements into one cohesive and easy-to-understand reference model. It categorizes the sections and chapters of the book into their specific areas of focus:

- **Align** - content aimed at aligning and harmonizing the organization around the concept of business intelligence
- **Define** - activity focused on requirements definition, associated business analysis, and the recommended action plan for delivering quick wins
- **Deliver** - content important to the successful delivery of quick wins
- **Reference** - supplemental reference material helpful to ensuring overall success

The model also distinguishes the methods you use in your requirements workshop from the methods designed for business analysis.

Finally, while this book shows you how you can accelerate the value of business intelligence through organizational alignment, right requirements, and quick wins, it is not a technical resource on how to architect, deploy, or govern a BI solution. The Hyper Framework does illustrate, though, the place where agile delivery fits into the process.

ALIGN

Requirements Workshop Part I

Section 1 - Understanding BI

Chapter 1 - Value Creation

Chapter 2 - The BI Value Chain

Chapter 3 - Value Enablers

Chapter 4 - The Problem with BI

Section 2 - The Imperatives for Success

Chapter 5 - Addressing the Problem with BI

Chapter 6 - Unify

Chapter 7 - Simplify

Chapter 8 - Amplify

Chapter 9 - Qualify

Chapter 10 - The Importance of Collaboration

DEFINE

Requirements Workshop Part II

Section 3 - Methods to Accelerate Planning

Chapter 11 - Building Requirements for Quick
Wins and Beyond

Chapter 12 - Painting the Big Picture

Chapter 13 - Prioritizing Misson-Critical
Information Needs

Chapter 14 - Building the Information Universe

Business Analysis

Chapter 15 - Validating the Information Model

Chapter 16 - Bridging the Gap Between Business
and IT

Chapter 17 - Mapping the Data

Chapter 18 - Creating the Execution Plan

Chapter 19 - Documenting Your Findings

DELIVER

Section 4 - Ways to Accelerate Execution

Chapter 20 - Be Quick and Nimble

Chapter 21 - Socialize, Market and Sell

Chapter 22 - Monitor, Evaluate and Evolve

Chapter 23 - Bringing It All Together

Agile Delivery

Design, Develop and Test

Deploy and Train

Integrate and Iterate

REFERENCE

Section 5 - Beyond Planning and Execution

Chapter 24 - Effective Group Facilitation

Chapter 25 - Thoughts On Information Delivery

Chapter 26 - Another Perspective on Big Data

Chapter 27 - Working with Consultants

Chapter 28 - Characteristics of a Hyper Mindset

Chapter 29 - A Final Word

Appendix - Recommended Resources

Figure 13 – Hyper Framework

SECTION 5
BEYOND PLANNING AND EXECUTION

Ever wonder why Forrester Research suggests that "Only the bravest should dive into BI programs without professional help"?[1] Because delivering a BI capability that really works is tough and often requires a level of know-how that only comes with years of practical experience. This book is designed to help accelerate your understanding of proven practices and field-tested methods to help increase your likelihood of success.

In this section, I present some thoughts and offer-up some tips on additional items that are just as important but are rarely addressed.

CHAPTER 24
EFFECTIVE GROUP FACILITATION

" Think about what it takes to lead 100 musicians to make beautiful music together. Or how much sensitivity it takes to understand why people behave the way they do. While the qualities that separate a great conductor or therapist from a mediocre one may be subtle, the outcomes are obvious. The same holds true for facilitators.[1] "

- Bob Zimmerman

EFFECTIVE GROUP FACILITATION

Do you consider yourself a great facilitator? If so, how do you know?

I ask the question because the process of facilitating your requirements workshop is arguably the most important part of planning and execution. This workshop is where you align and harmonize the thinking of your key stakeholders. It's where you uncover business pain and the information decision-makers need to eliminate it. And it's the all-important place where you begin to set and manage expectations. Get the workshop wrong and you're in a heap of trouble.

Getting the most out of your requirements workshop requires a great facilitator—someone who, as Bob Zimmerman puts it, is "part business analyst, part orchestra conductor, and part psychologist."[2] A tall order, no doubt. But if you're someone who is serious about delivering a BI capability that helps move the needle in business performance, you need to take the role seriously.

Here are my top tips on effective group facilitation.

Group Facilitation Tip #1 – Be prepared

Nothing sets a negative tone worse than a facilitator who isn't prepared. To kick things off in a positive way:

- Know your audience. From the spelling and pronunciation of their names to political dynamics and pet peeves, know who they are and what they do

- Know the subject matter your audience cares about

- Never make your audience wait. You should have your workshop environment set-up and waiting for your audience to arrive—pads, pencils, table tents and water bottles at each seat, the projector on, your welcome slide up, phone working, and coffee hot. Greet attendees as they arrive

- Start on time

Group Facilitation Tip #2 – Set clear expectations

After your ice breaker and introductions, set clear expectations for the day. Talk about the agenda and what you plan to accomplish. Be sure to cover meeting ground rules so everyone knows what behavior is acceptable and what is not.

Group Facilitation Tip #3 – Manage the workshop

It's the facilitator's job to keep the audience on topic and on time while getting the most out of group dynamics. A great facilitator knows when to push participants past unproductive discussion, and he knows when to let productive conversations run long in order to drive maximum results from the stakeholder workshop.

Group Facilitation Tip #4 – Encourage and challenge

Often times workshop participants need help articulating their ideas. Encourage them by using phrases like, "Tell me more…" or "Expand on that." Don't always take a comment or an opinion as the only truth. When appropriate, challenge your participants to think through their ideas by asking, "Why is that?" or "Do others see it that way?" When you encounter an ambiguous comment, seek clarity by restating it and asking for feedback. Use comments like, "This is what I heard…" or "State that another way for me." Encourage and challenge by actively engaging.

Group Facilitation Tip #5 – Document everything

The requirements workshop provides you with a unique opportunity to gather your key stakeholders together in one place at the same time. Document everything so you don't lose important and relevant context. If your audience is comfortable with the idea, record the session. Always have an experienced scribe on-hand to capture session notes electronically. And make maximum use of easel pads. When the workshop is over, you can peel the sheets from the wall, roll them up, and take them with you for additional review and analysis.

CHAPTER 25
THOUGHTS ON INFORMATION DELIVERY

❝ Most dashboards that are used in businesses today fail.[1] ❞

- Stephen Few

THOUGHTS ON INFORMATION DELIVERY

I saw a number of recent postings circulating on LinkedIn with an unattributed graphic that read:

> *"A user interface is like a joke. If you have to explain it, it's not that good."*

Amen to that.

Now that you've worked your way through the Quick Wins Model—educated and aligned stakeholders, gathered requirements, and prepared data for your first quick win—it's time to focus on information delivery. I can tell you from experience that the value your stakeholders ultimately place on any quick win is directly tied to how well (and fast!) your delivery method supports their need for actionable insight. The last thing you want to do is fall flat.

So, I recommend the use of an interactive dashboard for the successful delivery of quick wins. Stephen Few, educator and founder of Perceptual Edge, defines a dashboard as a "visual display of the most important information needed to achieve one or more objectives; consolidated and arranged on a single screen so the information can be monitored at a glance." It is, as he explains, "...a unique and powerful solution to an organization's need for information,"[2] and I agree.

You can create a dashboard quickly using any number of advanced data visualization tools on the market, and an interactive dashboard enables you to effectively set and manage end-user expectations around self-service analytics.

Creating a dashboard that works, however, takes education and discipline—and that's why so many of them used in business today fall flat on expectations. Too many practitioners responsible for BI delivery think 3D pie charts are cool, and they love traffic lights, meters, and cute little gauges. But, as Mr. Few points out, "An effective dashboard [is really the result] of informed design: more science than art, more simplicity than dazzle. It is, above all else, about communication."[3] To work, a dashboard must engage your audience, leave an impression, and get them to take action.[4]

Here are a few tips to help get you there.

Information Delivery Tip #1 – Understand best practices

Take the time to educate and inform yourself on visual design practices for interactive dashboards. Start with anything from Stephen Few. He's written several books including his most recent, *Information Dashboard Design: Displaying data for at-a-glance monitoring*. In addition, his site contains a wealth of information on best practices including valuable "before and after" illustrations.[5] Same thing with Wayne Eckerson and the research and consulting experts at Eckerson Group.[6] And be sure to check out the work of a firm called Juice Analytics.

Its team recently authored an interesting and valuable book called, *Data Fluency: Empowering your organization with effective data communication.*[7]

Information Delivery Tip #2 – Establish and adhere to standards

Once you know how to design a dashboard that works, establish your own standards, practices, guidelines, and templates you can easily reuse and repeat from one quick win to another. Save yourself a lot of headaches by prohibiting "rogue" developers to stray from your documented policies.

Information Delivery Tip #3 – Keep it simple

When it comes to dashboard design, less is definitely more. Don't overdo it. Remember that "Elegance in communication is often achieved through simplicity of design."[8]

CHAPTER 26
ANOTHER PERSPECTIVE ON BIG DATA

" Between now and 2020, the amount of digital information created and replicated in the world will grow to an almost inconceivable 35 trillion gigabytes as all major forms of media—voice, TV, radio, print—complete the journey from analog to digital.[1] "

- Gantz and Reinsel

ANOTHER PERSPECTIVE ON BIG DATA

According to IBM, we're creating 2.5 quintillion bytes of data each and every day—"so much that 90% of the data in the world today has been created in the last two years alone."[2] The ever- increasing volume and detail of data from global financial systems, web-based retail transactions, social media chatter, the growing expanse of digital everything, and a myriad of other sources have propelled us into the era of "big data." It's the latest and greatest technology trend and an exciting one at that.

In an O'Reilly Radar post called "An Introduction to the Big Data Landscape," technologist and writer Edd Dumbill defines the catch-all term "big data" as "data that exceeds the processing capacity of conventional database systems."[3] Big data is data that originates from sources like personal and corporate email, automobile sensors, XML feeds, Apache weblogs, online purchases, and the growing expanse of digital everything. Its sheer volume, velocity, and variety make big data different from anything most organizations have ever had to deal with from an information management perspective. As Dumbill accurately points out, "big data" is either too big, moves too fast, or doesn't always look like the kind of data we're used to putting into our corporate databases, so we have to choose alternative ways to process and store it if we stand any chance of finding value in it.[4]

For forward-looking business leaders, the value of big data lies in the promise of new discovery and insight that can fuel greater operational performance—not from traditional business intelligence, but from an emerging and related discipline Dumbill calls "data science": the merging of "math, programming, and scientific instinct."[5] Big data evangelists relish the prospect of answering questions that, in the past, were simply beyond reach.

In its report entitled, "Big Data: The Next Frontier for Innovation, Competition, and Productivity,"[6] the McKinsey Global Institute presents five ways organizations can use big data to create value:

- By making information transparent and usable at a much higher frequency

- By collecting more accurate and detailed performance information on everything from product inventories to sick days

- By allowing ever-narrower segmentation of customers

- By enabling sophisticated analytics that can substantially improve decision-making

- By improving the development of next-generation products and services

McKinsey believes that big data will become a key basis of competition and growth and will underpin new waves of productivity. "From the standpoint of competitiveness and the potential capture of value," the firm writes, "all companies need to take big data seriously. In most industries, established competitors and new entrants alike will leverage data-driven strategies to innovate, compete, and capture value from deep and up-to-real-time information."[7]

The New York Times cited a recent World Economic Forum report entitled "Big Data, Big Impact" that declares data "a new class of economic asset, like currency or gold."[8] Gartner says that "'Big data' initiatives create significant opportunities for business and IT leaders...."[9] And Forrester analyst Vanessa Alvarez sums it all up by simply stating, "Big data means big value."[10]

So, to a lot of people, big data is a really big deal.

Here's the thing.

In a study conducted by Accenture, 53 percent of the middle managers say that less than half of the information they receive on a routine basis today through traditional BI channels is even valuable, and 42 percent say that at least once a week they inadvertently use the wrong information to guide decisions.[11] For far too many executives, right information is either incomplete or missing entirely from the decision-making process. Unlike those evangelists who see new and endless possibilities in big data, most of the executives I work with relish the prospect of using the data they already have to answer basic questions around operational performance to drive value.

In my view, big data should only be a big deal for organizations already experienced in using information to better manage and optimize the enterprise. For them, big data provides a big opportunity for discovery and insight that can drive incredible innovation. Everyone else should keep big data on their radar but focus first on building a BI competency that is hyper-responsive, hyper-agile, and hyper-flexible.

CHAPTER 27
WORKING WITH CONSULTANTS

" A consultant's job is to make you look good—to make sure you're better off now than you were when he first arrived. "

WORKING WITH CONSULTANTS

Not long ago I read a thought-provoking article in *Harvard Business Review* entitled, "A Consultant's Guide to Firing a Client."[1] Written by Dorie Clark—a marketing strategist, author, and professional speaker who teaches at Duke University's Fuqua School of Business, the piece focuses on when and how to end an unproductive consulting relationship. As a long-time consultant who's had his share of tough situations, I found the article intriguing.

In fact, the commentary really got me thinking about why tough situations occur, the role both parties play, and what a client can do to prevent an unproductive consulting relationship. After all, no client wants to be fired by his consultant. It's bad for everyone. So, consider this chapter "A Client's Guide to Keeping a Consultant."

Years ago, McKinsey & Company conducted a study[2] to determine why organizations hire consultants in the first place. Really, not much has changed:

- Consultants provide competencies not readily available elsewhere
- They offer varied experience gained outside of the client's industry
- Consultants have time to study the problem.
- They are professionals
- They are independent

- Consultants have the ability to create action based on recommendations they make

In a nutshell, consultants fill critical gaps in thought-leadership, skills, and capabilities and ultimately help businesses overcome the kind of people, process, and technology barriers that can block an organization's forward progress. And that's a good and worthy and mutually-beneficial thing until perception, fear, tradition, or ignorance clouds the attitude, behavior, thinking, or judgment of client personnel that typically surfaces through:

- Whispered discontent
- Quietly second-guessing decisions
- Undermining work effort
- Failing to communicate or miscommunicating on purpose
- Deflecting responsibility by pointing fingers

Understand that when engaging a client, a consultant has three primary objectives:

1) A consultant wants to be your trusted advisor
2) A consultant wants to build a long-term relationship
3) A consultant wants you as a reference

When you consider the significance of the objectives, you should quickly realize that negative attitudes and unproductive behavior are all an unnecessary waste of energy.

CHAPTER 27

A consultant's job is to make you look good—to make sure you're better off now than you were when he first arrived. A consultant succeeds when you succeed.

As a client, you can build a strong, healthy consulting relationship by following these four simple tips:

Healthy Relationship Tip #1 - Build rapport
Google defines rapport as "a close and harmonious relationship in which the people or groups concerned understand each other's feelings or ideas and communicate well."[3] Synonyms include affinity, understanding, and empathy. You and the consultant are a team, and mutual respect is important for mutual success.

Healthy Relationship Tip #2 - Don't be hyper-sensitive
No one is out to get you, overshadow you, or take your job; so, focus your time and energy on things that matter. Don't cling too tightly to your own ideas. When a consultant challenges your thinking, be open-minded; and never be shy about challenging back!

Healthy Relationship Tip #3 - Empower your partner
Unlike the consultant, you already have in-depth knowledge of your organization—goals and objectives, policies, procedures, standards, people, systems, data, and politics. You've also built your own intellectual capital from practical, hands-on experience. A consultant is your partner. Take the time to educate and inform him. Empower him to do the best job he can so that he can help make you successful.

Healthy Relationship Tip #4 - Listen and learn

Because of their cross-industry experience, broad-based knowledge, and subject matter expertise, experienced consultants provide you with a unique opportunity to learn. Take advantage of it (I certainly do!). Listen, observe, and ask lots of questions. Absorb as much as you can. You never know what the future holds.

CHAPTER 28
CHARACTERISTICS OF A HYPER MINDSET

" Batman is...the most 'realistic' of the great superheroes. To be blunt: the guy isn't very super. He didn't gain his powers by being lightning-struck, nor bathing in chemicals, nor by dint of being born on another planet, nor by the intervention of extraterrestrials or gods. To paraphrase an old commercial, he got them the old-fashioned way—he earned them...He wasn't bequeathed those abilities; he sweated for them.[1] "

- Dennis O'Neil

CHARACTERISTICS OF A HYPER MINDSET

In my experience, a Hyper mindset is a unique type of mindset. In fact, I often consider someone who does exhibit it as a sort of business superhero—an ordinary person with an extraordinary attitude. Someone with a passion for the possible and an unrelenting will to do transformative work.

We often relate the concept of a superhero to our favorite cartoon character or some masked avenger who uses superhuman power to fight crime on the streets of a big city. The business superhero isn't that kind of guy. He's more like Batman—described by comic book artist Neal Adams as the only superhero who really isn't a superhero at all. "He has no powers," writes Adams. "He's [simply] a human being bent on a mission."[2] This describes someone with a Hyper mindset.

"Batman is an ordinary mortal who made himself a superhero," writes Jenette Kahn, former president and editor-in-chief of DC Comics. "Through discipline and determination and commitment, he made himself into the best."[3]

In a posting for Startup America Partnership, Jason Nazar, co-founder and CEO of Docstoc.com, identifies "10 Traits Entrepreneurs Share with Superheroes."[4] They are also the 10 characteristics that I believe can turn any ordinary mortal into a "human being bent on a mission."

They represent the best characteristics of a Hyper mindset:

1) A superhero never gives up. He overcomes challenges by wholeheartedly committing to unrelenting persistence

2) A superhero always gets the job done. There are no excuses. You either save the day or you don't

3) A superhero is the best at what he does. He excels in areas where his superpowers are needed most

4) A superhero is crystal clear in his purpose. He's always focused and results-oriented

5) A superhero recognizes his flaws. The goal in anything he does isn't perfection. It's the pursuit of perfection

6) A superhero doesn't seek glory. He does what he does because it's the right thing to do

7) A superhero helps others. He's never obsessed with himself but with helping other people solve problems

8) A superhero is more powerful when he's part of a team of superheroes. When you're taking on the world, help is vital

9) A superhero knows that true strength comes from his character. He's always courageous, respectful, honorable, and selfless

10) A superhero accomplishes great feats. Failure is never an option

Do some or all of these characteristics describe you? Be disciplined, determined, and committed to developing a Hyper mindset. "Find that bit of Batman within and have the will to put it to good use."[5] Go and make a superhero of yourself. Your organization needs you.

CHAPTER 29
A FINAL WORD

" None of us is as smart as all of us.[1] **"**

- Ken Blanchard

A FINAL WORD

I am a firm believer in the synergistic power of the group and the value of the intellectual capital that results from effective collaboration. We all have different skills and capabilities and diverse backgrounds and experiences that form our perspectives and the way we approach our work. Some of mine are reflected in this book.

Now I'd like to hear from you!

Tell me what you think of Hyper. Does the material resonate with you? How has your experience differed from mine — or has it? Have you established your own tried-and-true methods for requirements-gathering? What challenges have you faced trying to make BI work? How have you overcome them?

Let's talk about it. Send your thoughts to me at HyperTheBook@steffine.com. And don't forget to connect with me on LinkedIn at www.linkedin.com/in/steffine.

In the meantime, please tell others what you think of my book by leaving a review on Amazon. Word-of-mouth is crucial for any author to succeed. Even a sentence or two can make an important difference.

BONUS MATERIAL

The Hyper Toolkit

Join my mailing list at www.steffine.com and receive the same Microsoft® Visio, Microsoft® Word, and Microsoft® Excel templates I use to create many of the documents I describe in this book. They are great tools you can customize and use to jump-start your own work. It's my way of saying thanks.

You will need to enter the order number from your book purchase to qualify for this complimentary offer. This material is delivered electronically through email.

APPENDIX – RECOMMENDED RESOURCES

This series of books offers various perspectives on business, business intelligence, and value creation. They are from some of my favorite authors, and I reference a number of them in this book.

Analytics At Work: Smarter Decision, Better Results
Davenport, Thomas H., Jeanne G. Harris, and Robert Morison. *Analytics at Work: Smarter Decisions, Better Results.* Boston, MA: Harvard Business, 2010.

Big Data @ Work: Dispelling the Myths, Uncovering the Opportunities
Davenport, Thomas H. *Big Data @ Work: Dispelling the Myths, Uncovering the Opportunities.* Harvard Business School, 2014.

Big Data: Using Smart Big Data, Analytics and Metrics to Make Better Decisions and Improve Performance
Marr, Bernard. *Big Data: Using Smart Big Data, Analytics and Metrics to Make Better Decisions and Improve Performance.* Chichester: Wiley, 2015.

Business Intelligence for Dummies
Scheps, Swain. *Business Intelligence for Dummies.* Hoboken, NJ: Wiley, 2008.

Competing on Analytics: The New Science of Winning

Davenport, Thomas H., and Jeanne G. Harris. *Competing on Analytics: The New Science of Winning.* Boston, Mass.: Harvard Business School, 2007.

How to Become a Rainmaker: The Rules for Getting and Keeping Customers and Clients

Fox, Jeffrey J. *How to Become a Rainmaker: the Rules for Getting and Keeping Customers and Clients.* New York: Hyperion, 2014.

Information Dashboard Design: Displaying Data for At-A-Glance Monitoring

Few, Stephen. *Information Dashboard Design: Displaying Data for At-A-Glance Monitoring.* 2nd ed. Burlingame, Calif.: Analytics, 2013.

It's Not the Big That Eat the Small...It's the Fast That Eat the Slow

Jennings, Jason, and Laurence Haughton. *It's Not the Big That Eat the Small...It's the Fast That Eat the Slow.* HarperCollins, 2002.

Mastering the Rockefeller Habits: What You Must Do to Increase the Value of Your Growing Firm

Harnish, Verne. *Mastering the Rockefeller Habits: What You Must Do to Increase the Value of Your Growing Firm.* New York: Gazelles, 2002.

Now You See It: Simple Visualization Techniques for Quantitative Analysis

Few, Stephen. *Now You See It: Simple Visualization Techniques for Quantitative Analysis.* Oakland, Calif.: Analytics, 2009.

Performance Dashboards: Measuring, Monitoring, and Managing Your Business

Eckerson, Wayne W. *Performance Dashboards: Measuring, Monitoring, and Managing Your Business.* Hoboken, N.J.: John Wiley, 2006.

Positively Outrageous Service: How to Delight and Astound Your Customers and Win Them for Life

Gross, T. Scott. *Positively Outrageous Service: How to Delight and Astound Your Customers and Win Them for Life.* 2nd ed. Chicago: Dearborn Trade Pub., 2004.

Secrets of Analytical Leaders

Eckerson, Wayne W. *Secrets of Analytical Leaders.* Westfield, NJ: Technics Publications, 2012.

Show Me the Numbers: Designing Tables and Graphs to Enlighten

Few, Stephen. *Show Me the Numbers: Designing Tables and Graphs to Enlighten.* Oakland, Calif.: Analytics, 2004.

Simple: Conquering the Crisis of Complexity

Siegel, Alan. *Simple: Conquering the Crisis of Complexity.* S.l.: Grand Central, 2013.

Sticky Wisdom: How to Start a Creative Revolution at Work

Rudkin, Daz. *What If!, Sticky Wisdom: How to Start a Creative Revolution at Work.* 2nd ed. Oxford: Capstone, 2002.

Strategy Maps: Converting Intangible Assets Into Tangible Outcomes

Kaplan, Robert S., and David P. Norton. *Strategy Maps: Converting Intangible Assets Into Tangible Outcomes.* Boston: Harvard Business School, 2004.

Successful Business Intelligence: Secrets to Making BI a Killer App

Howson, Cindi. *Successful Business Intelligence: Secrets to Making BI a Killer App.* New York: McGraw-Hill, 2008.

Successful Business Intelligence: Unlock the Value of BI & Big Data

Howson, Cindi. *Successful Business Intelligence: Unlock the Value of BI & Big Data.* 2nd ed. New York: McGraw-Hill Education, 2014.

The 4 Disciplines of Execution: Achieving Your Wildly Important Goals

McChesney, Chris, and Sean Covey. *The 4 Disciplines of Execution: Achieving Your Wildly Important Goals.* New York: Free Press, 2012.

The Difference Maker: Making Your Attitude Your Greatest Asset.

Maxwell, John C. *The Difference Maker: Making Your Attitude Your Greatest Asset.*
Nashville: Nelson Business, 2006.

The Five Dysfunctions of a Team: A Leadership Fable

Lencioni, Patrick. *The Five Dysfunctions of a Team: A Leadership Fable.* San Francisco: Jossey-Bass, 2002.

The Intelligent Company: Five Steps to Success with Evidence-Based Management

Marr, Bernard. *The Intelligent Company: Five Steps to Success with Evidence-based Management.* Chichester, West Sussex, U.K.: John Wiley & Sons, 2010.

The Lexus and the Olive Tree: Understanding Globalization

Friedman, Thomas L. *The Lexus and the Olive Tree.* New York: New York: Picador, 2012.

The New Know: Innovation Powered by Analytics

May, Thornton A. *The New Know: Innovation Powered by Analytics.* Hoboken, N.J.: Wiley, 2009.

The Profit Impact of Business Intelligence

Williams, Steve, and Nancy Williams. *The Profit Impact of Business Intelligence.* Amsterdam: Elsevier/Morgan Kaufmann, 2007.

The Value Factor: How Global Leaders Use Information for Growth and Competitive Advantage
Hurd, Mark, and Lars Nyberg. *The Value Factor How Global Leaders Use Information for Growth and Competitive Advantage.* Princeton: Bloomberg, 2004.

Thinking for a Change: 11 Ways Highly Successful People Approach Life and Work
Maxwell, John C. *Thinking for a Change: 11 Ways Highly Successful People Approach Life and Work.* New York: Warner, 2003.

Thriving on Chaos: Handbook for a Management Revolution
Peters, Thomas J. *Thriving on Chaos: Handbook for a Management Revolution.* New York: Knopf, 1987.

The following websites are excellent resources on business intelligence, analytics, and big data. Several have channels relating to specific topics like data science, data discovery, master data management, and information strategy, among others. Refer to them often.

BeyeNETWORK	b-eye-network.com
CIO	cio.com
CFO	cfo.com
Information Week	informationweek.com
Information Management	information-management.com
TechTarget	techtarget.com/network
Big Data University	bigdatauniversity.com
Massive Open Online Courses (MOOC) on Big Data	mooc-list.com/tags/big-data

Look to the research community for unbiased perspectives on business intelligence, analytics, and big data.

Business Application Research Center (BARC)	barc-research.com
Dresner Advisory Services	dresneradvisory.com
Forrester Research, Inc.	forrester.com
Gartner, Inc.	gartner.com
Info-Tech Research	infotech.com
International Data Corporation	idc.com
The Economist Intelligence Unit	economistinsights.com

Supplement the knowledge you gain from the research community with insight and lessons learned from some of the largest professional services organizations in the world.

Accenture   accenture.com

Bain & Company   bain.com

Deloitte   deloitte.com

Ernst & Young   ey.com

IBM   ibm.com

KPMG   kpmg.com

McKinsey & Company   mckinsey.com

PricewaterhouseCoopers (PwC)   pwc.com

Specialists in business intelligence, big data, and analytics can often provide the thought-leadership, innovative ideas, and best practices you need to be successful.

AlyData	alydata.com
Dahlem & Associates	dahlemassociates.com
Eckerson Group	eckerson.com
Juice Analytics	juiceanalytics.com
Perceptual Edge	perceptualedge.com
simpleBI	simplebi.com
The Data Governance Institute	datagovernance.com
The Data Warehousing Institute	tdwi.org

NOTES

FOREWORD

[1] McNabb, Kyle, Josh Bernoff, Cliff Condon, Et.al. "The CIO's Blueprint For Strategy In The Age Of The Customer: Four Imperatives To Establish New Competitive Advantage." *Forrester Research, Inc.*, 12 Sep. 2014. (http://goo.gl/W5MsjK).

[2] Le Clair, Craig, Christopher Mines, Alex Cullen, and Julian Keenan. "Business Agility Drives Higher Performance: Channel Integration Is The Most Important Dimension Of Agility." *Forrester Research, Inc.*, 12 Nov. 2013. (http://goo.gl/ZddVos).

[3] Evelson, Boris, Holger Kisker, Martha Bennett, and Nasry Angel. "It's Time For A User-Driven Enterprise BI Strategy." *Forrester Research, Inc.*, 25 Aug. 2014. (http://goo.gl/aY7scD).

[4] Evelson, Boris, Holger Kisker, Martha Bennett, Et.al. "Build An Agile BI Organization." *Forrester Research, Inc.*, 5 Feb. 2015. (http://goo.gl/6lIHsR).

[5] Evelson, Boris, Holger Kisker, Martha Bennett, and Nasry Angel. "The Forrester Wave™: Agile Business Intelligence Platforms, Q3 2014: The 16 Providers That Matter Most And How They Stack Up." *Forrester Research, Inc.*, 3 Jul. 2014. (http://goo.gl/3EYD4m.)

[6] "The Business Intelligence Playbook For 2015: Grow Your Business And Compete By Creating A Winning Business Intelligence Strategy." *Forrester Research, Inc.*, 2015. (http://goo.gl/B21esu).

PREFACE

[1] May, Thornton A. *The New Know: Innovation Powered by Analytics.* Hoboken, N.J.: Wiley, 2009.

[2] "The Value Habit: A Practical Guide for Creating Value." Straight Talk Book No. 6. Deloitte Development LLC. (2005).

[3] *Hyper-.* (http://goo.gl/2lAJo6).

[4] *Responsive.* (http://goo.gl/XPIJWT).

[5] *Agile.* (http://goo.gl/3G0yTD).

[6] *Flexible.* (http://goo.gl/blPYKN).

SECTION 1
[1] Hurd, Mark, and Lars Nyberg. *The Value Factor: How Global Leaders Use Information for Growth and Competitive Advantage.* Princeton: Bloomberg, 2004.

CHAPTER 1
[1] "Value Creation: The Ultimate Measure by Which a Company Is Judged." *The Economist.* 20 Nov. 2009. (http://goo.gl/hDmXgo).

[2] Prahalad, C. K., and Venkat Ramaswamy. *"Co-Creation Experiences: The Next Practice in Value."* 2004. (http://goo.gl/9GNXu6).

[3] "CIOs Name BI and Analytics No. 1 Investment Priority for 2015." *KDnuggets.* 1 Jan. 2015. (http://goo.gl/Dylwbj).

[4] Schmid, Beth. "Freeman: Business Is About Creating Value Together." *UVA Today.* 10 June 2010. (http://goo.gl/9Zyr7K).

[5] Porter, Michael E. "Doing Well at Doing Good: Do You Have a Strategy?" *Global Leadership Summit,* Willow Creek Association, South Barrington, IL, August 10, 2007.

CHAPTER 2

[1] Konrath, Jill. *Value Proposition Generator* (http://goo.gl/3BYFCM).

[2] Ernst & Young. "Lessons from Change: Findings from the Market." *EYGM Limited*, 2010. (http://goo.gl/g73XMR).

[3] Friedman, Thomas L. *The Lexus and the Olive Tree: Understanding Globalization*. New York: Picador, 2012.

[4] Jennings, Jason, and Laurence Haughton. *It's Not the Big That Eat the Small...It's the Fast That Eat the Slow*. HarperCollins, 2002.

CHAPTER 3

[1] Davenport, Thomas. "Competing on Analytics." *Harvard Business Review*. Jan. 2006. (http://goo.gl/hXEdju).

[2] *Decision support tools: Porter's value chain*. (http://goo.gl/MzsgEO).

[3] Porter, Michael E. *Competitive Advantage: Creating and Sustaining Superior Performance*. Kindle ed. New York: Free, 2008.

[4] Davenport, Thomas. "How Organizations Make Better Decisions." *International Institute for Analytics*, 1 Jan. 2010. (http://goo.gl/as8fZ2).

[5] Griffin, Jane. "Putting the Business Back into Business Intelligence Initiatives." *Information Management* RSS. 5 Mar. 2007. (http://goo.gl/Tq0HCl).

[6] Davenport, "How Organizations Make Better Decisions."

CHAPTER 4

[1] Harris, Jeanne. "Insight-to-Action Loop: Theory to Practice." *Accenture Research Note* (2005).

[2] Ulrich, David, and John H. Zenger. *Results-based Leadership.* Boston: Harvard Business School, 1999.

[3] Martens, China. "BI at Age 17." *Computerworld.* 23 Oct. 2006. (http://goo.gl/ZQf4Sq).

[4] May, Thornton A. *The New Know: Innovation Powered by Analytics.* Hoboken, N.J.: Wiley, 2009.

CHAPTER 5

[1] "Boris Evelson's Blog." Trends 2011 And Beyond: Business Intelligence. 3 Nov. 2011. (http://goo.gl/IEK3EV).

CHAPTER 6

[1] "The Quotations Page: Quote from John Lilly." *The Quotations Page.* (http://goo.gl/KP1mOY).

[2] "Businesses failing to Understand Business Intelligence." *Computing News.* 18 Jan. 2007. (http://goo.gl/niNDuc).

[3] Daniel, Diann. "10 Keys to a Successful Business Intelligence Strategy." *CIO.* 22 Oct. 2007. (http://goo.gl/kGk69s).

[4] Davenport, Thomas, Don Cohen, and Al Jacobson. "Competing on Analytics." *Babson Executive Education*, May 2005. (http://goo.gl/lo5eYn).

[5] "Strategic BI and Competency Plans Are Key to Success Says Gartner." *Computing.* 31 Jan. 2007. (http://goo.gl/1DbSrm).

[6] "Albert Einstein Quote." *Quote DB.* (http://goo.gl/JpGC3R).

[7] Pentilla, C. "I Know Too Much." *Entrepreneur* 1 Feb. 2007.

[8] Gingrich, Newt, and Nancy Desmond. *The Art of Transformation.* CHT Press, 2006.

[9] "Zig Ziglar Quote." *BrainyQuote.* Xplore. (http://goo.gl/Fucc2O).

[10] Maxwell, John C. *The Difference Maker: Making Your Attitude Your Greatest Asset.* Nashville: Nelson Business, 2006.

[11] Gingrich and Desmond, *The Art of Transformation.*

CHAPTER 7

[1] "E. F. Schumacher Quote." *BrainyQuote.* Xplore. (http://goo.gl/HAPLfE).

[2] Siegel, Alan. *Simple: Conquering the Crisis of Complexity.* S.l.: Grand Central, 2013.

[3] Ibid.

[4] Howson, Cindi. *Successful Business Intelligence: Unlock the Value of BI & Big Data.* 2nd ed. New York: McGraw-Hill Education, 2014.

[5] Bennett, Martha, and Boris Evelson. "Forrester: Best Practice Tips for Business Intelligence Success." *ComputerWeekly.com.* 1 Aug. 2013. (http://goo.gl/Yb6CQh).

CHAPTER 8

[1] Clarry, Maureen. "Business Intelligence Results Yield Business Wisdom." *BeyeNETWORK.* 21 July 2009. (http://goo.gl/33vgt7).

[2] Ibid.

[3] Kawasaki, Guy. *Selling the Dream: How to Promote Your Product, Company, or Ideas, and Make a Difference, Using Everyday Evangelism.* New York, N.Y.: HarperCollins, 1991.

[4] "CIO Q&A: The Business Case for Business Intelligence | Insurance & Technology." *Insurance & Technology.* (http://goo.gl/RC44jy).

[5] Roach, Dale. *Like A Team.* (http://goo.gl/N6436b).

CHAPTER 9

[1] "Above the Fray." *BI and Beyond Sharing the Intelligence.* SAS.com, 2005. (http://goo.gl/nNY3hd).

[2] "Almost a Third of BI Projects Fail to Deliver on Business Objectives." *ComputerWeekly.com.* 10 Jan. 2012. (http://goo.gl/THDZeT).

[3] Ibid.

[4] "Business Intelligence Offers the Promise of Widespread Benefits, Yet Many Challenges Remain." *PRNewswire.* (http://goo.gl/6ZE2Sm).

[5] "Pervasive BI Still Elusive, Survey Reveals." *TDWI.* 29 Jan. 2013. (http://goo.gl/I228zp).

[6] Clarry, "Business Intelligence Results Yield Business Wisdom." *BeyeNETWORK.* 21 July 2009. (http://goo.gl/33vgt7).

[7] Ibid.

CHAPTER 10

[1] "Philosophy 101: Importance of Collaboration." (http://goo.gl/wGHLfa).

[2] "A Quote by Kenneth H. Blanchard." *Goodreads.* (http://goo.gl/pp9LFR).

[3] Richardson, Adam. "Collaboration Is a Team Sport, and You Need to Warm Up." *Harvard Business Review.* 31 May 2011. (http://goo.gl/xouuvL).

[4] "Chapter 2: Global E-business and Collaboration." (http://goo.gl/88OUvb).

[5] Schutte, Bart. "Effective Collaboration Leads to Better Performance (part 1)." *Recent Posts*. 16 Mar. 2011. (http://goo.gl/h02mus).

[6] Davenport, Thomas H., and Jeanne G. Harris. *Competing on Analytics: The New Science of Winning*. Boston, Mass.: Harvard Business School, 2007.

[7] Created by author courtesy of The Project Cartoon.com Beta. (http://goo.gl/AVG99c).

[8] Krivada, Cheryl. "Becoming an Analytical Competitor." *Teradata Magazine Online - Vol. 7, No. 2*. June 2007. (http://goo.gl/nb6MMq).

CHAPTER 11

[1] "Strategies for Project Recovery: A PM Solutions Research Report." *PM Solutions Research*, 2011. (http://goo.gl/melC4G).

[2] Leffingwell, D. "Calculating Your Return on Investment from More Effective Requirements Management." *IBM - United States*. 1996. (http://goo.gl/TtHcgq).

[3] "The CHAOS Report." *The Standish Group*, 2014. (http://goo.gl/9CRLLJ).

[4] "Getting Smart About BI: Best Practices Deliver Real Value." *BusinessWeek Research Services*, Sept. 2006. (http://goo.gl/rSUdWR).

CHAPTER 12

[1] Drucker, Peter F. *Management: Tasks, Responsibilities, Practices*. New York, Harper & Row, 1974.

[2] "Alvin Toffler Quote." *BrainyQuote*. Xplore. (http://goo.gl/bu2upy).

[3] Pratt, Mary. "Extreme BI." *Computerworld*. 4 June 2012. (http://goo.gl/fTrqEd).

[4] Pettey, Christy. "Gartner Says Organizations Spend Less Than 30 Percent of Their Time, Energy and Money on Technology Issues Related to Business Intelligence." 13 Mar. 2007. (http://goo.gl/DnKd9x).

[5] "Blue sky." (http://goo.gl/Vzp46m).

CHAPTER 13

[1] Myers, Randy. "IQ Matters: Boosting Information Quality -." *CFO*. 6 Mar. 2006. (http://goo.gl/aBnFVC).

CHAPTER 14

[1] Connelly, Richard, Robin McNeill, and Roland Mosimann. The *Multidimensional Manager: 24 Ways to Impact Your Bottom Line in 90 Days*. Cognos Incorporated, 2001.

[2] Ibid.

[3] Ibid.

[4] "Measure." *BusinessDictionary.com*. (http://goo.gl/UrSk7F).

[5] "Dimension." *SearchDataManagement*. (http://goo.gl/0px2A1).

[6] "Drilling down, up, and across." *Kimball Group*. (http://goo.gl/neNHLR).

[7] "Hierarchies." (http://goo.gl/j0DiHB).

[8] "Dimensions, Levels, and Attributes." (http://goo.gl/iHZP0I).

CHAPTER 15

[1] "Data-Driven: The New CFO/CIO Dynamic." *CFO Insights* (2012). (http://goo.gl/ZnyT1m).

CHAPTER 16

[1] Gainer, Jeff. "Manage Your Users by Managing Expectations." *Enterprise Development.* 1999. (http://goo.gl/iyxAiV).

[2] "Schemas." (http://goo.gl/QdLWxT).

CHAPTER 17

[1] Simms, Jed. "Why Projects Fail: Part Two, Poor Business Requirements." *CIO.* 26 June 2007. (http://goo.gl/ukeBV6).

[2] Williams, Steve, and Nancy Williams. *The Profit Impact of Business Intelligence.* Amsterdam: Elsevier/Morgan Kaufmann, 2007.

[3] Ibid.

[4] "Value chain." (http://goo.gl/eshZRb).

CHAPTER 18

[1] Nunns, James. "Self-Service Reporting Is Biggest Big Data Challenge." *Computer Business Review.* 30 Jan. 2015. (http://goo.gl/Q6xq5W).

SECTION 4

[1] Scheps, Swain. *Business Intelligence for Dummies.* Hoboken, NJ: Wiley, 2008.

CHAPTER 20

[1] Clive, Tom. "The Importance of Business Agility." *The Huffington Post.* 24 Apr. 2013. (http://goo.gl/n8wWj1).

[2] Howson, Cindi. "Tableau: On a Mission for Everyone to See and Understand Data." *BI Scorecard*. 15 Sept. 2014. (http://goo.gl/16Ew1M).

[3] "Nimble; The New Big." Ascent Advising. (http://goo.gl/8bgKGa).

[4] "The Twelve Principles of Agile Software." Agile Alliance. (http://goo.gl/EymP1H).

[5] "5 Factors In Agile BI." *InformationWeek*, 1 Jun. 2011. (http://goo.gl/N1cFKs).

CHAPTER 21

[1] "Technology evangelist." *Wikipedia*. Wikimedia Foundation. (http://goo.gl/QNyBPH).

[2] Geller, Lois. "Why A Brand Matters." *Forbes*. 23 May 2012. (http://goo.gl/ZCt66T).

CHAPTER 22

[1] Evelson, Boris, Holger Kisker, Martha Bennett, and Nasry Angel. "Grow Your Business And Compete By Creating A Winning Business Intelligence Strategy." *Forrester Research, Inc.*, 25 Nov. 2014. (http://goo.gl/pP2mwx).

[2] Weinzimmer, Larry, and Jim McConoughey. "Failure Is The Only Option, If Success Is The End Goal." *Fast Company*. 7 Sept. 2012. (http://goo.gl/MWqGmk).

[3] Howson, Cindi. "BI Adoption Flat." *BI Scorecard*. 7 Apr. 2014. (http://goo.gl/QL9id8).

[4] Bennett, Martha, Boris Evelson, Holger Kisker, and Carmen Stoica. "BI On BI: How To Manage The Performance Of BI Initiatives." *Forrester Research, Inc.*, 22 Dec. 2014. (http://goo.gl/mtGIFN).

[5] Evelson, Boris. "Agile BI Ship Has Sailed--Get On Board Quickly Or Risk Falling Behind." *Boris Evelson's Blog. Forrester Research, Inc.*, 3 July 2014. (http://goo.gl/Nml1fY).

[6] Evelson, Boris. "BI on BI Or How BI Pros Must Eat Their Own Dog Food." *Boris Evelson's Blog. Forrester Research, Inc.*, 5 May 2013. (http://goo.gl/kaZwlp).

[7] Ibid.

[8] Bennett, "BI On BI: How To Manage The Performance Of BI Initiatives."

SECTION 5
[1] Evelson, Boris, and Liz Herbert. "The Forrester Wave™: Business Intelligence Services Providers, Q4 2012." *Forrester Research, Inc., 18 Oct. 2012. (http://goo.gl/nPH5Bg).*

CHAPTER 24
[1] Zimmerman, Bob. "The Great Facilitator." *BA Times.com.* 3 Jan. 2012. (http://goo.gl/qrsXcv).

[2] Ibid.

CHAPTER 25
[1] Few, Stephen. *Information Dashboard Design: The Effective Visual Communication of Data.* Beijing: O'Reilly, 2006.

[2] Ibid.

[3] Ibid.

[4] Halper, Fern. "Telling a Story with Analysis: 3 Visualization Tips for Presenters." TDWI, 2 Dec. 2014. (http://goo.gl/l4aGJa).

[5] Visit http://goo.gl/3xu7lb to learn more.

[6] Visit http://goo.gl/OeghjT to learn more.

[7] Gemignani, Zach, and Chris Gemignani. Data Fluency Empowering Your Organization with Effective Data Communication. Indianapolis, IN: John Wiley & Sons, 2014.

[8] Bennett, "BI On BI: How To Manage The Performance of BI Initiatives."

CHAPTER 26

[1] Gantz, John, and David Reinsel. "The Digital Universe Decade – Are You Ready?" *IDC*, May 2010. (http://goo.gl/UEM9YH).

[2] "Bringing Big Data to the Enterprise: What is Big Data?" *IBM - Big Data At the Speed of Business.* 21 Mar. 2015. (http://goo.gl/7ZAyXq).

[3] Dumbill, Edd. "What Is Big Data?" *O'Reilly Radar.* 11 Jan. 2012. (http://goo.gl/tavBmM).

[4] Ibid.

[5] Ibid

[6] Manyika, James, Michael Chui, Brad Brown, Jacques Bughin, Richard Dodds, Charles Roxburgh, and Angela Hung Byers. "Big Data: The Next Frontier for Innovation, Competition, and Productivity." *McKinsey & Company,* May 2011. (http://goo.gl/3OoVsc).

[7] Ibid.

[8] Lohr, Steve. "The Age of Big Data." *The New York Times.* 11 Feb. 2012. (http://goo.gl/JSS6AI).

[9] "From Data to Decision: Delivering Value from 'Big Data.'"
From Data to Business Discovery, Issue 1. *QlikTech,* Jan. 2012.

[10] Kerner, S.M. "Forrester analyst: Big data isn't about size #Interop."
(http://goo.gl/zK1pok).

[11] "Managers say the majority of information obtained for their work is useless, Accenture survey finds." *Accenture Newsroom.* 4 Jan. 2007. (http://goo.gl/YlAfxB).

CHAPTER 27

[1] Clark, Dorie. "A Consultant's Guide to Firing a Client."
Harvard Business Review. 26 Jan. 2015. (http://goo.gl/k5P7oU).

[2] Appelbaum, Steven H., and Anthony J. Steed. "The Critical Success Factors in the Client-consulting Relationship." *Journal of Management Development* 24.1 (2005): 68-93. (http://goo.gl/D5ckpw).

[3] "Rapport." (http://goo.gl/ux04mz).

CHAPTER 28

[1] Zehr, E. Paul. "Why Does Batman Matter?" *Psychology Today*, 2 Mar. 2012. (http://goo.gl/C0ktdr).

[2] Zehr, E. Paul. *Becoming Batman: The Possibility of a Superhero.* The Johns Hopkins University Press, 2008.

[3] Zehr, "Why Does Batman Matter?"

[4] Nazar, Jason. "10 Traits Entrepreneurs Share With Superheroes." Startup America Partnership. 21 Mar. 2015. (http://goo.gl/tLYSPC).

[5] Zehr, E. Paul. "Why Does Batman Matter?" Psychology Today, 2 Mar. 2012.

CHAPTER 29

[1]"A Quote by Kenneth H. Blanchard." Goodreads. (http://goo.gl/usyreh).

INDEX

"f" denotes figures

CPSIA information can be obtained at www.ICGtesting.com
Printed in the USA
BVOW06*1908260715

409492BV00001B/1/P

9 780692 459263